D0979047

Praise for *The Jesuits*

"Only John W. O'Malley is today in a position to offer a sweeping scholarly yet accessible overview of the extraordinarily rich and complex history of the Society of Jesus—from Ignatius of Loyola to Pope Francis."

—**Robert A. Maryks, Boston College, editor in chief of the** *Journal of Jesuits Studies*

"John O'Malley's brief history of the Jesuits is both readable and accurate. From the order's official foundation by the Basque nobleman Ignatius of Loyola in 1540 to the recent election of a Jesuit pope, the story of the Jesuit order as told here is one of extraordinary consistency, flexibility, and persistence. O'Malley provides a dispassionate account of the role of Jesuit education throughout the world, and of the often violent political reactions to the order's perceived power. Readers will be inspired to follow up on the more detailed sources listed here, but John O'Malley's text stands alone as an authoritative and illuminating guide."

—**Elizabeth Cropper, dean, Center for Advanced Study in the Visual Arts, National Gallery of Art**

THE JESUITS

A History from Ignatius to the Present

JOHN W. O'MALLEY, SJ

A Sheed & Ward Book

ROWMAN & LITTLEFIELD
Lanham • Boulder • New York • Toronto • London

Published by Rowman & Littlefield
A wholly owned subsidary of The Rowman & Littlefield
Publishing Group, Inc.
4501 Forbes Boulevard, Suite 200, Lanham, Maryland 20706
www.rowman.com

16 Carlisle Street, London W1D 3BT, United Kingdom

Distributed by NATIONAL BOOK NETWORK

British Library Cataloguing in Publication Information Available

Library of Congress Cataloging-in-Publication Data

O'Malley, John W.
  The Jesuits : a history from Ignatius to the present / John W. O'Malley, SJ.
    pages cm
  "A Sheed & Ward Book."
  Includes bibliographical references and index.
  ISBN 978-1-4422-3475-8 (cloth : alk. paper)—ISBN 978-1-4422-3476-5
(electronic) 1. Jesuits—History. I. Title.
BX3706.3.O425   2014
271'.53—dc23

                                                      2014007970

Printed in the United States of America

CONTENTS

IMPORTANT DATES IN
THE HISTORY OF THE
SOCIETY OF JESUS

1491 Birth of Ignatius of Loyola

1521 Battle of Pamplona, where Ignatius was wounded and his conversion begun

1534 Ignatius and six fellow students at the University of Paris pronounce a vow to go to Jerusalem

1540 Official approval of the Society of Jesus by Pope Paul III

1542 Francis Xavier arrives in India

1547 Portuguese Jesuits arrive in Brazil

1548 Jesuits open their school in Messina, Italy

1556 Ignatius dies in Rome

1558 The First General Congregation approves the *Constitutions* and elects Diego Laínez to succeed Ignatius

1583 Matteo Ricci and Michele Ruggieri enter China

1614 Jesuits and other missionaries expelled from Japan
      Publication of the *Monita Secreta*

1622 Canonization of Ignatius and Xavier

1656 Pascal publishes the first of his *Provincial Letters*
1704 Condemnation of "Chinese Rites" by Pope Clement XI
1754 Outbreak of the "War of the Seven Reductions"
1759 Expulsion of the Jesuits from Portugal and Portuguese dominions
1764 King Louis XV issues the royal decree suppressing the Jesuits in France
1767 Jesuits suppressed in Spain and Spanish dominions and their properties seized
1773 Worldwide suppression by Pope Clement XIV, *Dominus ac Redemptor*
1801 Pope Pius VII validates the existence of the Society in Russia, *Catholicae fidei*
1814 Worldwide restoration of the Society by Pius VII, *Sollicitudo omnium ecclesiarum*
1965 Election of Pedro Arrupe as superior general, Thirty-First General Congregation
2013 Election of Jorge Mario Bergoglio as Pope Francis, the first Jesuit pope

PREFACE

Within a few decades the Society of Jesus will observe the five hundredth anniversary of its founding in 1540. During the course of almost five centuries, it has had a rich, complex, and often tumultuous history. Much admired and much reviled, it has from the beginning eluded facile categorization. On the most basic level, the Society is simply a Roman Catholic religious order, whose members pronounce the traditional vows of poverty, chastity, and obedience. Like the members of other orders, the Jesuits engage in the traditional ministries of preaching and administering the sacraments. Like the members of many orders, Jesuits travel as missionaries to distant lands and peoples. "The world is our house," as Jerónimo Nadal, an early and extremely influential Jesuit, put it.[1]

About a decade after their founding, however, the Jesuits began to operate schools for lay students, something no religious order had ever done before in a systemic way. At that point they began to assume a profile that was altogether distinctive. Through the schools they were drawn into aspects of secular culture in ways and to a degree unprecedented for a religious order. Jesuits became poets, astronomers, architects, anthropologists, theatrical entrepreneurs, and much more.

They were much appreciated. They were also feared and hated, even by many Catholics. Histories written about them have for centuries reflected this bifurcation: the Jesuits were saints; the Jesuits were devils. Of course, there were always more judicious appraisals, but only about twenty years ago did an almost seismic shift occur as historians began approaching the Jesuits in a more even-handed way, asking the simple and neutral question, "What were they like?"

This approach has been extremely fruitful and has generated an unprecedented outpouring of studies on every aspect of the Jesuit enterprise. The quality of this new research is consistently high. We now know more about the Jesuits than ever before, and we see them in new and helpful perspectives.

The pages that follow are informed by that scholarship. In them I limit myself to two objectives: (1) to provide in almost skeletal form the basic narrative of the origin, development, triumphs, and tribulations of the Society of Jesus up to the present; (2) to provide through almost arbitrary choice descriptions in detail of a few undertakings—lest the narrative soar too high and lose touch with the concrete reality that is history. This small book will have been a success if it whets readers' appetites to read further into the fascinating history of the Jesuits.

1

FOUNDATIONS

On February 2, 1528, a devout Basque nobleman, Iñigo de Loyola, arrived in Paris. At the advanced age of thirty-seven, he intended to pursue a degree at the university. Iñigo enrolled in the Collège de Montaigu, where he remained for a year before transferring to the Collège Sainte-Barbe. At Sainte-Barbe he shared lodgings with two much younger students, Pierre Favre and Francisco Xavier. Friendships formed among them and then expanded to include four more students—Diego Laínez, Alfonso Salmerón, Nicolás Bobadilla, and Simão Rodrigues. At this time Iñigo began to refer to himself as Ignacio or Ignatius, the name by which he has been known ever since.

Inspired by Ignatius, these "friends in the Lord," as they described themselves, vowed in the summer of 1534 to travel together to the Holy Land to live at least for a while where Jesus lived and to work for "the good of souls." However, if because of the disturbed political situation in the Mediterranean they could not get passage, they would offer themselves to the pope for whatever ministries he thought best. On August 15 during a mass celebrated by Favre, the only priest among them at the time, they bound themselves to this course of action as well as to a life of poverty. Since they all in fact intended to be ordained, they were already committed to a life of celibate chastity. They did not realize at the time that on that fateful August 15, 1534, they took the first step that led six years later to the founding of the Society of Jesus.

Before these seven left Paris to begin their journey, they were joined by three more students—Claude Jay, Paschase Broët, and Jean Codure. By 1537 the ten, now holding their prestigious Master of Arts degrees from the University of Paris, had arrived in Venice. There they were ordained and awaited passage eastward. As they waited they engaged in preaching and other ministries in northern and central Italy. When asked who they were, they now responded that they were members of "a brotherhood of Jesus," in Italian *una compagnia di Gesù* (in Latin, *Societas Iesu*). As the months passed and turned into years, they realized that political tensions made the trip to the Holy Land impossible. What were they to do? Should they stay together, and even take more members into their *compagnia*? If so, should they go so far as to try to found a new religious order?

In the spring of 1539 they gathered in Rome. Over the course of three months they met almost daily to deliberate about their future. Not only did they quickly decide to stay together and found a new order, but as the weeks unfolded they were able to sketch the contours of the order in sufficient detail to submit their plan to the Holy See for approval. They called the document their *Formula vivendi*, their "plan of life." The Holy See, after raising questions, hesitating, and then making small modifications, accepted the *Formula* and incorporated it into the bull of approval signed by Pope Paul III, *Regimini militantis ecclesiae*. With the bull's publication on September 27, 1540, the Society of Jesus officially came into existence.

On April 19 the next year, the members elected Ignatius their first superior general, an office he held until his death in 1556. Even before the election was settled, Francisco Xavier was, at the behest of King John III of Portugal, already on his way to Lisbon to prepare for his departure as a missionary in India. He arrived at his overseas destination two years later to become the most famous missionary in modern times. While Xavier traveled beyond India to evangelize other parts of southeast Asia, Ignatius, by contrast, sat at his desk in Rome guiding the new Society, a task that included writing *Constitutions*, in which structures and procedures were spelled out in much greater detail than in the *Formula*.

From ten members in 1540, the Society grew at almost breathtaking speed to a thousand by the time Ignatius died sixteen years later. Except for the British Isles and Scandinavia, it had established itself in virtually every country of western Europe, in most of which it opened schools, already the Jesuits' trademark ministry. It had also established itself overseas. Of the thousand members in 1556, some fifty-five were in Goa in India and twenty-five in Brazil, where they had arrived in 1547. Two years later Xavier entered Japan, where he laid the groundwork for the Jesuits' most successful mission in the Far East. He died in 1552 on the verge of entering mainland China.

The Society of Jesus was only one of several new religious orders founded at about the same time, but it grew and achieved a status that far exceeded the others. The Theatines, founded in

1524, had by mid-century only thirty members, all of them in Italy. The Barnabites and Somascans had comparably small numbers, who also were all in Italy. How to explain this discrepancy?

THE SOCIETY OF JESUS TAKES SHAPE

When the ten founders drew up the *Formula*, they seemed to envisage the Society as an updated version of the so-called mendicant orders such as the Dominicans and Franciscans founded in the thirteenth century. They described themselves as engaging primarily in the same ministries of preaching and hearing confessions. They, like the Dominicans and Franciscans, saw these ministries as almost by definition itinerant and without geographical limits, which thus implicitly entailed overseas missions. They in fact conceived the Society as essentially a missionary order. In the *Formula* the founders made explicit their dedication to "missions anywhere in the world" by a special vow that obliged them to be ready to travel "among the Turks, or to the New World, or to the Lutherans, or to any others whether infidels or faithful." (Because this vow was in addition to the customary three of poverty, chastity, and obedience, it is commonly referred to as the Fourth Vow.) Although they specified the pope as the one who would send them on these missions, they soon realized this provision was impracticable, and in their *Constitutions* they invested the superior general with the primary responsibility in this regard. Nonetheless, the Jesuits and others came to interpret the vow as giving the Society a special relationship to the papacy. It was not, however, as it is often erroneously described, a vow of "loyalty to the pope." It was a vow to be missionaries.

Although the founders were all priests, within a few years the Jesuits, like the mendicants, made provision for nonordained members. At times in the history of the Society these "lay brothers" (or, better, temporal coadjutors, which is the Jesuits' official term for them) constituted about a third of the membership. They served the Society as cooks, buyers, and treasurers and in other practical tasks. Some were highly skilled professionals—architects, for instance, and artisans of various types. Among the more famous was the painter Andrea Pozzo (1642–1709), but there were others of extraordinary talent.

Even within the parameters of the *Formula*, the Jesuits made adjustments that set them off from their mendicant model, some of which shocked contemporaries and made the Jesuits suspect in their eyes. The Jesuits would not wear a distinctive religious habit, for instance, and they retained their family names. Instead of a set term of, say, three or six years, they elected their superior general for life and accorded him much more authority than did the mendicants. The name they insisted upon for themselves, the Society of Jesus, struck others as arrogant and self-serving.

Most controversial, however, was the provision in the *Formula* that the members not recite or chant the Liturgical Hours such as matins and vespers in choir, which up to that point was considered almost the definition of a religious order. By forgoing that traditional practice, which required members of the community to assemble for prayer several times a day, the founders argued that they had greater flexibility to meet the needs of ministry at whatever hour of day or night they occurred.

Such provisions, important though they were in the eyes of contemporaries, do not adequately explain why the Jesuits grew so rapidly and achieved such a distinctive culture. Other factors were more important, such as the international and cosmopolitan background of the original ten members and the prestige of their Paris degrees. Determinative, however, was the person of Ignatius, who influenced the Society in a number of ways, but perhaps nowhere more profoundly than as author of the *Spiritual Exercises*.

Born probably in 1491, Iñigo/Ignatius followed the usual course for a younger son in a family of his social class. When he was probably about seven, he left the family castle at Loyola to serve first as page and then as courtier in the household at Arévalo of Juan Velásquez de Cuéllar, chief treasurer of Castile. He remained there about ten years. At Arévalo he learned to dance, sing, duel, read and write Spanish, and get into brawls.

When Velásquez died in 1517, Ignatius entered the service of Don Antonio Manrique de Lara, duke of Nájera and viceroy of Navarre. When French forces invaded Navarre in 1521 and advanced on Pamplona, Ignatius was there to defend it. During the crucial battle, a cannonball shattered his right leg and damaged the left. The wound was serious, and despite several excruciatingly painful operations, it left him with a limp for the rest of his life.

He recuperated at his early home, the castle of Loyola. His religious conversion took place during those long months. He found at the castle none of the tales of chivalrous knights and their ladies that he loved to read and that might now relieve his boredom. In some desperation he turned to the only literature at hand—the *Life of Christ* by Ludolf of Saxony and excerpts from *The Golden Legend*, a medieval collection of lives of the saints. The latter led him to speculate about the possibility of fashioning his own life after the saints and of imitating their deeds.

In his imagination, however, he debated for a long time the alternatives of continuing according to his former path as courtier and soldier, even with his limp, or of turning completely from it to the patterns exemplified especially by Saint Dominic and Saint Francis of Assisi. He found that when he entertained the first alternative he was afterward left dry and agitated in spirit, whereas the second brought him serenity and comfort. By consulting his inner experience in this way, he gradually came to the conviction that God was speaking to him through it, and he finally resolved to begin an entirely new life. This process of self-examination by which he arrived at his decision became a distinctive feature of the way he would continue to govern himself and became a paradigm of what he would teach others.

Once his physical strength was sufficiently restored, he set out from Loyola on a pilgrimage to Jerusalem. On the way he planned to spend a few days at the small town of Manresa outside Barcelona to reflect upon his experience up to that point. For various reasons, including originally the outbreak of the plague, he prolonged his stay there for almost a year. He gave himself up to a severe regimen—long hours of prayer, fasting, self-flagellation, and other austerities that were extreme even for the sixteenth century. However, this program sent him into such a deep spiritual and psychological crisis that at one point he was tempted to suicide.

By attending once again to his inner inspiration, he began to find guidance. He greatly tempered his austerities and found that as a result his serenity of mind returned and he was more capable of helping others who came to him to "speak about the things of God," as he put it. He had reached a critical moment in his spiritual life that later had profound repercussions on the spirituality of the Society. He turned away from the model of sanctity that prevailed up to that time, which assumed that the more severely the body was punished, the better the soul would flourish. It assumed that the greater the withdrawal from "the world," the holier one would be.

Only in the light of this change at Manresa can we understand why Ignatius, as he returned from his pilgrimage to the Holy Land, decided to enter a university "the better to help souls." Only in the light of Manresa can we understand why, unlike all religious orders up to that time, the *Constitutions* professedly abstained from prescribing penances or austerities for the Jesuits and, indeed, went on to insist that "a proper care to preserve one's health and strength of body for God's service is praiseworthy and should be exercised by all" (#292). Only in the light of this change at Manresa can we understand how in the *Constitutions*, Ignatius could prescribe that, along with prayer and other spiritual means, Jesuits make use in their ministries of natural means: "Therefore the human or acquired means ought to be sought with diligence, especially well-grounded and solid learning . . . and the art of dealing and conversing with others" (#814). Not monastic silence was the ideal but cultivation of the art of conversation. A significant moment had been reached in the history of Catholic piety.

With his serenity returned, Ignatius began to receive great consolations of soul and internal enlightenment, which sometimes took the form of visions. In all this he became convinced God was gently teaching him and leading him along the right path. He made notes about what was transpiring in his own soul and what he observed taking place in others who came to speak with him. These notes contained some of the essential elements from which the *Spiritual Exercises* eventually emerged. The book was, thus, not a product of theory but of lived experience. Although Ignatius continued to revise the notes over the next twenty years, he had much of it fundamentally in hand when he left Manresa to complete his pilgrimage to Jerusalem.

The result was a book unlike any other up to that time, a manual of "exercises" and reflections to help individuals get in touch with themselves and with the action of God within them. As the text says, the goal was to create a situation where "the Creator deals directly with the creature, and the creature directly with his Creator and Lord" (#15). The *Exercises* are not, then, a book to be read but to be *used* so as gently to lead an individual along a spiritual path consonant with the person's gifts and personality.

Ignatius wrote the book while still a layman, and he intended it for anybody intent on a deeper spiritual life. Yet the book came to play a determining role in the ethos of the Jesuits themselves. In the *Constitutions* Ignatius prescribed that every novice entering the Society spend a full month making the *Exercises* (#65). The novice, it was hoped, would begin to develop a life of prayer that went far beyond rote recitation of prayers and formal observance of regulations and that brought him to a sense of intimacy with God. His commitment to the life he had chosen would be heartfelt, deep, and lifelong, no matter how difficult the circumstances in which he later found himself. At the time no other religious order had a program for its novices that was anything like it.

The *Spiritual Exercises* also delivered into the hands of the Jesuits a new ministry, which came to be called the "retreat." Of course, retirement from one's ordinary duties for prayer and reflection is older than Christianity itself, but the *Exercises* for the first time provided a structured yet flexible program for doing so. The Jesuits set to work putting this ministry into practice, and in 1553, for instance, they built at their college at Alcalá outside

Madrid a building specifically intended for housing men making the *Exercises*, the first of their many "retreat houses" around the world. More broadly, the *Exercises* helped the Jesuits see all their ministries as spiritual, ultimately aimed at leading others on a spiritual journey beyond routine of rite and ritual.

In the sixteenth century, the *Exercises* had severe critics who saw in them a dangerous form of mysticism that minimized or made irrelevant the sacraments and other usages of the church in favor of God's direct communication with the individual. Ignatius repeatedly had to defend their orthodoxy before the Inquisition in various cities until he finally arrived in Rome. Even after they were published in 1548 with the approbation of Pope Paul III, they were not immune from criticism and suspicion.

Important though the *Exercises* were in creating the identity of the Jesuits, they were not Ignatius's only service to the Society. He possessed a remarkable gift for leadership. Once he became superior general, the gift manifested itself especially in three ways. First, he displayed remarkable acuity in choosing two men to assist him in forming the Society. Their talents complemented his own and help account for the stability and esprit de corps remarkable for such a rapidly expanding and geographically sprawling enterprise as the Society of Jesus early became.

In choosing Juan Alfonso de Polanco as his secretary, he found a person of broad culture who at the same time showed a genius for organizing how the central office of the order could keep effectively in touch with members spread far and wide. In choosing Jerónimo Nadal as his "agent in the field," he found a man of extraordinary energy and persuasive powers who traveled across Europe visiting Jesuit communities, interviewing each member, and then explaining and exemplifying what it meant to be a Jesuit. The collaboration among these three men accounts for the cohesion and stability (amid much confusion!) that the new order enjoyed from the beginning.

Secondly, Ignatius, with the aid of Polanco, composed the Jesuit *Constitutions*, which broke new ground for the genre. Unlike the correlative documents of other orders, the *Constitutions* were not a simple collection of ordinances and regulations but a coherent presentation of ideals and goals. The originality of the *Constitutions* was nowhere more striking than in the developmental design according to which they followed the Jesuit from entrance into the Society through his training and commissioning for ministry. The final part of the *Constitutions* describes the qualities required in the superior general, which amounts to a portrait of the ideal Jesuit. It was a book, therefore, with beginning, middle, and end.

Like the *Exercises*, the *Constitutions* were based on a presupposition that psychological or spiritual growth will take place, and they provided for it by prescribing certain things as appropriate for beginners and suggesting others as appropriate for more seasoned members. In so doing the *Constitutions* evince a judicious mix of firmness and flexibility that allowed the Society to adapt to changing circumstances and still retain its identity. Undergirding it was an implicit theological assumption of the compatibility of Christianity with the best of secular culture, according to the axiom of Thomas Aquinas, the theologian the *Constitutions* prescribe for the order, that grace perfects nature. The Jesuit adoption of the axiom suggests, once again, the ongoing impact of Ignatius's "turn to the world" at Manresa.

Thirdly, Ignatius decided, after the Society had been in existence less than a decade, to commit it to the staffing and management of schools for young laymen, a bold new undertaking for a religious order. Leadership, though a gift difficult to analyze, certainly consists in large measure in vision, in the ability to see how at a given juncture change is more consistent with one's scope than staying the course. That is the quality Ignatius displayed at this juncture. The decision to found, staff, and operate schools meant that the Jesuits, while retaining their identity as missionaries, now also had an identity as resident schoolmasters. It was an identity not only not foreseen in the *Formula* but seemingly inconsistent with it. Somehow the Jesuits managed to hold the two ideals together.

The Jesuits now had a ministry that made them distinctive. They threw themselves into it unreservedly. By the time Ignatius died more than thirty schools were in operation, principally in Italy but also in other countries. Ten years later there were thirty in Italy alone but others in France, Germany, and elsewhere. Two, for instance, had just opened in Poland. Besides offering instruction, the schools served as excellent bases for other ministries. Moreover, the Jesuits discovered that the schools gave them access to a population, such as the parents of their students, that might not be attracted to their churches. The schools, some of which grew to physically imposing structures, developed into important civic institutions. They also immediately began to be a source of vocations to the Society and in that regard are among the principal factors in accounting for the Society's rapid growth and the high quality of the young men who entered it.

What moved Ignatius to this momentous decision? Many factors, surely. He came more and more to recognize the long-range advantages of ministry with a fixed base. He and his colleagues were, as university graduates, almost by definition committed to the "war against ignorance and superstition" that in the sixteenth century engaged both Protestants and Catholics. Moreover, he recognized that at Paris the first Jesuits had learned certain pedagogical techniques that made them particularly effective teachers.

The list of reasons could go on, but surely determinative for Ignatius was the philosophy of education that underlay the humanistic schools of the era. That philosophy, derived from classical antiquity but now revived and given a Christian cast by Renaissance theorists such as Erasmus, was radically student-centered. It promised to produce men of integrity, dedicated to the common good of church and society, and skilled in persuading others to similar dedication. That scope, Ignatius saw, coincided with the scope of the Society, and the schools provided a fine matrix for integrating the two.

Ignatius's decision inaugurated a new era in Roman Catholicism for formal education. If the Jesuits were the first religious order to undertake as a primary and self-standing ministry the operation of full-fledged schools for any students, lay or clerical, who chose to come to them, they were in time followed by many other orders, both male and female. Such schools became a hallmark of modern Catholicism in every part of the world. Their religious and cultural influence is beyond calculation.

Ignatius's decision had a transforming impact on the Society itself. Even in the early years the schools were comparatively large and complex institutions that required the best talent for their staffing, which meant that talent was not available for other ministries. The schools led the Jesuits into becoming major property owners. With their classrooms, theaters, courtyards, and astronomical observatories, they were often huge establishments, to which were attached a church and a Jesuit residence. In some places they became one of the most impressive monuments in the city. Then as now schools ate up money with seemingly insatiable appetites, which meant they were perpetually in debt and drove the Jesuits into undertaking a most mundane occupation, money raising. They thus in some quarters gained a reputation for being avid for gold.

Money raising was imperative because, as Ignatius told the Jesuits at Perugia in 1552, the schools were for "everybody, poor and rich."[1] They therefore charged no tuition. Since there was no income from the students, Jesuits had to look for funds elsewhere. As a result of sad experience, Ignatius began to insist that no school be opened unless its funding had been secured beforehand by endowment or some other means. Even when endowed, schools continued to need funds for operating expenses.

Although the program offered by the Jesuit schools held little appeal for many students from the lower social classes, the free tuition meant that in fact the schools attracted students from a range of socioeconomic backgrounds. In the Jesuit school in Munich between 1601 and 1776, for instance, about 5 percent of the students came from noble families, about another 12 percent from families of civic office holders. Some 83 percent, therefore, came from the rest of society. Of the 1,500 students in the school at Billom in France, 7 percent were of the nobility, 9 percent from the bourgeoisie, 24 percent of minor officials' class, and the rest from lower classes. These figures are typical, except of course for the relatively few "Colleges of Nobles" that the Jesuits ran in some places.

From the beginning most of the Jesuit schools were "colleges," that is, schools that taught the so-called lower disciplines of literature, history, drama, and related subjects. Boys entered when they were about eight or ten years old and remained for seven or eight years. Once a boy had completed the program, at about age eighteen, his formal schooling ended. The colleges were not, therefore, preparation for further studies at a university, although of course if a young man now wanted to pursue the professional training in law, medicine, philosophy, or theology that universities offered, he was well prepared for it.

However, some Jesuit schools also taught the higher disciplines of philosophy and theology, and thus they themselves qualified as universities. Within a few years after opening in 1551, for example, the Roman College began teaching philosophy (principally the works of Aristotle) and theology and, despite its name, became a university and was empowered to offer university degrees. Only a few Jesuit universities taught law and medicine, the other two disciplines offered by universities.

Perhaps the most important change the schools wrought within the Society was, as mentioned, the new kind and degree of its members' engagement with secular culture. The Jesuits in their own training and in the training of others moved beyond the traditional clerical subjects of philosophy and theology. Central to the humanistic curriculum they taught in their colleges was literature as found in the pagan classics of ancient Greece and Rome. Homer and Virgil, Sophocles and Terrence, Thucydides and Livy, Demosthenes and Cicero—virtually every Jesuit taught these nonclerical texts at some point in his career. Literature included drama, which led the Jesuits into writing and staging plays, unheard of for a religious order until that time.

The plays often entailed music, which led the Jesuits to engage for the students a *maestro di cappella*, sometimes a musician as distinguished as Palestrina or, much later, Charpentier. The plays almost as often entailed dance, which meant engaging a *maestro di ballo*. In 1688 the French Jesuit Claude-François Menestrier, sometimes considered the first historian of ballet, published his important *Des ballets anciens et modernes*. The Collège Louis-le-Grand in Paris became famous for its dance performances, which were attended by Louis XIV and the French aristocracy but were a scandal of worldliness for the Jesuits' enemies and critics.

Textbooks were needed at prices students could afford. In the last year of his life, Ignatius for that purpose had a printing press installed in the Roman College. One of the first books it produced was a Jesuit's edition of a pagan classic, Martial's *Epigrams*. By 1564 the press had acquired Arabic characters and by 1577, Hebrew. The Jesuits installed presses in other colleges, not without worry that they might seem to be running a business for profit. Although of modest dimensions, these presses performed important services for the Jesuits and their clients. In 1563, for instance, Nadal arranged for the press at the college in Vienna to print fifteen hundred copies of the *Spiritual Exercises*. In 1556 the Jesuits introduced printing in Goa. By means of it, the first book ever printed in India was Xavier's catechism.

Over the course of the centuries Jesuits produced an immense quantity of books on a wide variety of subjects, a phenomenon that became part of their corporate identity. As "ministers of the word," they like other Catholic priests wrote books on religious and theological subjects. But by force of their vocation as teachers of the humanities and "natural philosophy" (the forerunner of

modern science), the Jesuits wrote extensively and most character-
istically on those subjects as well, and they thereby developed a
profile that, in comparison with other orders, looked decidedly
secular.

THEIR MINISTRIES

The importance for the Society of the *Formula* that the original
ten members composed in 1539 and that was approved by the
papacy in 1540 can hardly be exaggerated. It was then and is now
the charter allowing the Jesuits to operate within the Catholic
Church. As long as the Society adheres to the basic principles of
the *Formula*, it is, at least theoretically, free to make its own decisions. A slightly revised version was solemnly approved by Pope
Julius III in 1550 and is the version still in force today.

Among its remarkable features is the clear definition of the
purpose of the Society, "the progress of souls in Christian life and
doctrine and the propagation of the faith." The "progress of souls"
meant doing ministry and "propagation of the faith" meant being
missionaries. In other words, the Society was founded for ministry,
especially in a missionary mode. Obvious though this might seem
to us today, it was not obvious to all those who wanted to join the
Society in its early years. Nadal, the first great rhetorician of the
Jesuit ethos, was forced to repeat again and again in his exhorta-
tions to fledgling Jesuit communities across Europe, "We are not
monks!"

The *Formula* was typically precise in listing the ministries the
Jesuits would exercise, a list that was expanded in 1550. "Ministry
of the word of God" held pride of place, a reflection of the fact

that since the founding of the mendicant orders in the thirteenth century, preaching had experienced an astounding revival that continued unabated into the sixteenth. The Jesuits understood this ministry in the broadest possible sense. First of all, of course, they engaged in preaching, not only in churches but on street corners and wherever they might be able to gather a crowd.

As ministers of the word, the Jesuits also engaged in what they called "sacred lectures," which were in essence an early form of adult education. They consisted in a series of lectures on a given topic, often a book of the Bible, that, for instance, might extend over the course of the Sunday and Wednesday afternoons during Lent. The Jesuit sat somewhere in the body of the church, with the congregation seated in front of him. He lectured on a subject such as the Epistle to the Romans, the Sermon on the Mount, or the Beatitudes, and took up where he had left off the previous day. Members of the congregation might take notes to help them remember what they were being taught. Once the Jesuits had their own churches, they engaged assiduously in these lectures, which are one of the most important and virtually forgotten aspects of Catholic life in the early modern period.

As ministers of the Word, the Jesuits from the beginning engaged in various forms of catechesis with both children and adults, and they devised imaginative ways to make the lessons attractive, such as setting them to verse or to popular tunes. One of the most distinctive pastoral strategies devised in Catholicism at the time was the so-called mission to small villages and hamlets. These missions, which were led by a team of three or four Jesuits and might last a week or longer, incorporated a carefully designed program of preaching, catechesis, confession, and the establishment or reform of an organization among the locals that would try to keep the enthusiasm alive once the missionaries left.

After ministries of the Word in the *Formula* came administering the sacraments, which for the Jesuits meant especially hearing confessions and distributing Holy Communion. Then came the corporal works of mercy such as acting as chaplains in prisons and hospitals, which in the history of the Society were much more important than is generally recognized. The list ended with the all-inclusive category: ". . . and any other works of charity according to what will seem expedient for the glory of God and the common good."

Not even the 1550 version of the text mentions the schools. That ministry was in its infant stages at the time, and the overwhelming importance it was soon to assume was not yet recognized. Experience outpaced text. This striking omission in the papal bull stands as a warning of the limitations of normative documents in trying to understand the Jesuits. It is imperative to go beyond them to see how the Jesuits put norms into practice—or ignored or went beyond them.

THE FIRST YEARS

Even before Paul III's approval of the Society, young men were knocking at the door seeking admission. By 1549 Jesuits lived and worked in twenty-two cities but had houses of their own in only seven—Goa, Lisbon, Coimbra, Gandia, Rome, Padua, and Messina. Many more sprang up in the next year, especially in Spain. The Jesuits had meanwhile entered Brazil, India, and Japan. In 1552 alone, eleven new colleges were opened, including one north of the Alps, in Vienna.

As the numbers grew, Ignatius followed the example of older orders and divided the Society into provinces, each headed by a superior known as the provincial who had oversight of the various Jesuit communities in the area he governed. By the middle of 1553, six provinces were in full operation—Aragon, Brazil, Castile, India, Italy, and Portugal. Shortly thereafter six more were added—Andalusia, France, Sicily, Ethiopia, and Upper and Lower Germany, but the Ethiopian province existed only on paper. The most prosperous province in numbers and prestige was Portugal, due largely to the favor of King John III. The king of Spain, Philip II, was cooler toward this new order, but that did not prevent, after a slow start, a considerable influx of members.

The largest single concentration of Jesuits was in Rome, where in 1555 some 180 lived, largely because the Roman College, founded just three years earlier, had already become a premier school for the training of Jesuits themselves on an international basis. The Roman College was, however, also on the road to becoming the school of choice for the sons of aristocratic families who did not envisage for themselves an ecclesiastical career. Its reputation for academic excellence soon outstripped that of the older University of Rome, the *Sapienza*.

One of the great ironies in the early history of the Jesuits is that, although they became known as "the shock-troops of the Counter-Reformation," the Reformation was for almost a decade peripheral to their concerns. Of course, from the beginning they opposed "Lutheranism," as they designated virtually every kind of Protestantism, and they worked against it wherever they happened to find it. Their primary focus, however, was elsewhere—on overseas missions and on the Mediterranean lands from which most of them came. They continued to assign a high priority to the missions, but especially in northern Europe they gradually began to focus more and more on combating the Reformation.

In 1543 a young Dutch student of theology at the University of Cologne named Peter Canisius entered the Society. A few years later Ignatius sent him to Messina as a member of the ten-man team that there founded the first Jesuit school. Then in 1550 he sent him, along with Jay and Salmerón, to the University of Ingolstadt. That was a turning point. For all practical purposes Canisius, who did not die until 1597, never again left "German lands." In no other part of Europe did the Society owe its success and identity so manifestly to a single individual, and in no other part of Europe did the Jesuits come to play such a pivotal role in determining the character of modern Catholicism.

Another turning point occurred in 1555. At the request of Pope Julius III, Ignatius dispatched Laínez and Nadal to the Diet of Augsburg. It was the first time Nadal had set foot in Germany. He was utterly dismayed at what he found. His sense of disaster was only intensified by the terms of the Peace of Augsburg that made Lutheranism legal in those parts of the Empire where the local ruler willed it to be so—*cuius regio, eius religio.* From that moment forward he labored with all his might to make Germany a special priority among his brethren in southern Europe. "Woe to us," he wrote, "if we do not help Germany."[2]

In that same year, Ignatius named Canisius the first provincial of a German province. Canisius took up the cause with utter dedication and began to dun Ignatius and his successors for reinforcements. Meanwhile, first as a small trickle but then in some numbers, Germans began to enter the order. Under Canisius's leadership the Jesuits engaged in controversy with Lutherans, but their main effort was with Catholics. In that regard they took the long view in seeing the schools as the key factor in preparing future generations—laymen who would be both devout and well educated.

During his long lifetime, Canisius himself was directly or indirectly responsible for the founding of eighteen Jesuit schools. This included a college in Prague, which in 1556 opened with twelve Jesuits, who were almost immediately joined by thirteen more. When Canisius visited Poland a few years later, he was just as appalled by the situation there as Nadal had earlier been in Germany. The Reformation had made such great inroads, especially among the nobility, that the country seemed inexorably destined to become Protestant. Nine years later, at the invitation of Cardinal Stanislaus Hosius, the Jesuits opened a school in Braniewo (Braunsberg) and shortly thereafter another in Pułtusk (Pułtask), some miles north of Warsaw. From that point forward they played a crucial role in the reestablishment of Catholicism in Poland.

But overseas missions held greater attraction for Jesuits from the Mediterranean world than did Germany. Nadal spurred them on by his explanations of the missionary character of the Fourth Vow, in which he proclaimed, "The world is our house." It was not in the relative comfort of their communities that the Jesuits should find themselves most at home, he said, but "when they are constantly on the move, when they travel throughout the earth . . . only let them strive in some small way to imitate Christ Jesus, who had nowhere on which to lay his head and who spent all his years of preaching in journey."[3]

At this point the Jesuits were having their best success in Brazil, due in the first place to the superior of the mission, the talented and energetic Portuguese nobleman Manuel da Nóbrega. Within two weeks of his arrival in Bahia de todos os Santos in 1549, he had organized children of the Portuguese colonists and natives into catechism classes that included singing and learning to read and write. Among the early Jesuits in Brazil, however, none was more important than José de Anchieta, a badly crippled nineteen-year-old Basque, who arrived in 1553. He became the energy center for Jesuit work among the natives, with whom he labored until his death forty-four years later. He had hardly set foot on Brazilian soil before he had composed a rough draft of a grammar in Latin characters of the Tupi language. His skill in rhyme and verse enabled him to set Christian beliefs to native tunes and to capitalize on the Indians' marvelous musical talent.

Not all the Jesuits were as skilled linguists as Anchieta, which posed a problem especially in hearing confessions of the Indians whom they had converted. They soon devised a practical solution by training boys to act as interpreters: penitents told their sins to the boy, who in turn related them to the Jesuit, and the boy then related back to the penitents what the Jesuit said. The bishop objected, but Nóbrega countered that the boys were well trained and scrupulous about keeping secret what they heard. The bishop would have been shocked had he heard that the Jesuits occasionally used Brazilian women for this task, about one of whom a Jesuit wrote in 1552, "I think she is a better confessor than I am."[4]

But here, as elsewhere, native customs challenged the Jesuits and left them unsure how to proceed. They soon realized, for instance, that the Indians had no idea of marriage as a stable and monogamous union and that both men and women changed partners frequently and capriciously. They became extremely cautious, therefore, about admitting adult Brazilians to baptism and adamant about not admitting them to the Society. But despite such problems, they laid the foundations for perhaps the most enduringly successful of the Jesuits' overseas missions. Except for Goa, other missions in the East were, at best, inchoate, and not until a few decades later would Philip II allow the Jesuits to enter Spanish America.

Despite the many successes the Society achieved during these early years, difficulties and problems abounded. In almost every way, for instance, the Jesuits were unprepared to open in rapid-fire fashion so many schools. The schools were too many, the Jesuits too few. Some Jesuits performed poorly in the classroom, while others protested they did not enter the Society to spend their lives teaching Latin grammar to adolescent boys. Local schoolmasters threw obstacles in their path, and, as mentioned, funding was never sufficient. Schools opened, but, sometimes hardly opened, they closed.

In time the Jesuits took steps to ensure adequate resources for prospective schools, and the situation improved. But they faced other internal problems. In Portugal Simão Rodrigues's governance of the province proved arbitrary, and Ignatius had to remove from office this old companion from student days in Paris, one of the original ten founders. Rodrigues resented how he had been treated and never quite forgave Ignatius. Meanwhile, Nicolás Bobadilla, another of the original "friends in the Lord," made known his displeasure in the authority Ignatius granted to Polanco and Nadal, and he took it upon himself to complain to the pope about Ignatius's "tyranny" in governing the Society.

The Jesuits in the meantime suffered criticism and attack from fellow Catholics, including bishops, because of their pastoral practices, none of which was more controversial in the sixteenth century than their advocacy of frequent reception of the Eucharist. In Spain they were criticized and decried for admitting "New Christians" into the Society, that is, Catholics of Jewish ancestry. No attack shocked them more, caused them greater dismay, and presaged more serious difficulties for them than the condemnation of the Society by the Faculty of Theology of the University of Paris.

In trying to establish itself in Paris, the Jesuits had made political miscalculations that set the bishop, the Parlement, and the Faculty against them. In the overheated political and religious atmosphere of the French capital, the Jesuits' mode of religious life was sufficiently untraditional to arouse fear and suspicion. On December 1, 1554, the Faculty of Theology, still considered the most prestigious in the Catholic world, published its decree, which concluded: "This Society appears to be a danger to the Faith, a disturber of the peace of the church, destructive of monastic life, and destined to cause havoc rather than edification." To its well-known condemnations of Erasmus and Luther, the Faculty now added the Jesuits.

The decree stunned the members of the Society, especially those who were graduates of the university. It was an extraordinarily serious blow to the reputation of this institution still in its infancy. Ignatius decided to react positively by seeking testimonials from around Europe about the good work the Jesuits were doing and the esteem in which they were held. A number of such letters flowed in, and they mitigated the sting. But the decree sowed suspicion of the Jesuits' orthodoxy, their style of life, and their pastoral practices that from this time forward they were never able fully to dispel.

In the face of such problems, the Jesuits found support from the highest possible authority, the papacy. In 1555, however, that source of security turned insecure when Giampietro Carafa became Pope Paul IV. Carafa, a reformer of fanatical zeal, distrusted all novelty and, because of Spanish occupation of his native

Naples for over a half century, nursed a deep antagonism for all things Spanish. He had many years earlier met Ignatius in Venice, and for reasons still obscure, the meeting had not gone well. According to a contemporary witness, when Ignatius heard of Paul's election as pope, he "shook in every bone in his body."[5]

Paul gave ear to Bobadilla's complaints about Ignatius, but not until a few months after his election did he show open hostility to the Society. Probably out of his chronic fear of Spanish conspiracies against him, he sent the papal police to search Jesuit headquarters in Rome for weapons, of which of course they found none. It was, however, only after Ignatius's death the next year when the First General Congregation met to elect his successor that the relationship with the pope devolved into a full crisis. Paul demanded that the new general's term be limited to three years instead of for life, and he imposed upon the Jesuits the daily obligation to chant the Liturgical Hours in choir.

The Jesuits had no choice but to comply. When Paul died in 1559, however, Diego Laínez, who succeeded Ignatius as general, followed the opinion of the canon lawyers he consulted that, since the pope's action regarding the Hours was at variance with the *Formula*, it was valid only during his lifetime unless the next pope solemnly insisted upon it. The new pope, Pius IV, did not insist and, moreover, issued a formal abrogation of Paul's limitation of the general's term. The crisis was thus overcome. For the next two centuries, although the Jesuits experienced difficult moments with the successors of Saint Peter, they by and large enjoyed their favor and found in them protection from their enemies.

2

THE FIRST HUNDRED
YEARS

In 1640 the Jesuits celebrated their first centenary. The provinces around the world entered enthusiastically into the occasion. Their superior general, Muzio Vitelleschi, exhorted them to use the occasion to thank God for what in the past hundred years he had wrought through the Society. The Jesuits indeed had much to be thankful for. Historians often describe the mid-seventeenth century as the high-water mark of Jesuit influence and success, after which such troubles began to afflict the Society that the eighteenth century was for them "the century of calamities," which culminated in 1773 with Pope Clement XIV's worldwide suppression of the order.

No doubt, by 1640 the Jesuits were widely influential in the world of culture and religion. Admired and sought after, they moved with seemingly equal ease among the highest and the lowest strata of society. Although they aroused distrust and resentment in certain quarters of the church, they for the most part seemed to be doing very well indeed. They were roundly hated and feared by Protestants, which for most Catholics was a sign the Jesuits were doing their job.

At the time of the centenary, there were about sixteen thousand Jesuits. They were divided into some forty provinces—five, for instance, in France; four each in Italy and Spain; three in Germany; two each in India and Sicily. Provinces were now further organized into so-called assistancies according to certain common traits such as language or geographical proximity. The French provinces, for instance, formed the French assistancy. However, assistancies were purely an organizational convenience. It was the provincials who singly or acting as a group made binding decisions within an assistancy. The superior general always had the last word—and sometimes of course the first word.

The number of Jesuits per province varied, but European provinces tended to have around five or six hundred members. According to a survey in 1626, the Peruvian and Mexican provinces were relatively large among those outside Europe, with 390 and 365 Jesuits respectively. In that same year, the Goa province had 320 members, the Philippines 128, but the vice-province of China only 30. The Flemish province with 860 members in 1640 competed with the Roman province for the title as the largest in the order. The Walloon province was not far behind.

Provinces typically contained, besides a few simple residences and a novitiate, a considerable number of colleges in proportion to the number of Jesuits. The colleges were by far the largest institutions in the provinces and, as mentioned, were the base for other ministries besides teaching. Smaller colleges might enroll barely a hundred students, the larger ones a thousand or more. Almost inevitably it seems, some larger colleges evolved into universities by offering programs in philosophy and, less often, theology.

Not counting the colleges in Rome itself, the Roman province in 1640 operated twenty-five—in Tivoli, Perugia, Florence, Ancona, and so forth in an area corresponding to the Papal States and the Grand Duchy of Florence. In the five provinces of France, the Jesuits ran about seventy colleges, and about ninety in the German assistancy, which included Austria and Bohemia. Each of the two Belgian provinces operated eighteen, which was an astounding concentration for such a small area. Outside Europe there were thirteen colleges in Mexico, for instance; eleven in Peru; and nine in Goa.

Such figures are approximate because of the variety of institutions sometimes designated as colleges and because at a rate difficult to track schools opened and others closed. They in any case reveal how massive the Jesuits' commitment to education was and how well established the Society had become in urban centers even outside Europe. Both the school and the church attached to a college nurtured the development of Marian congregations serving students and various groupings of adults. These congregations, also known as sodalities, were the Jesuit adaptation of lay brotherhoods or confraternities so popular in Catholic Europe since the late Middle Ages. Their purpose was, in the first place, to sustain the members' religious devotion, but the congregations also often engaged in works of social assistance to the needy and in sponsoring cultural events such as concerts and oratorios. The Jesuits founded them in every place they labored.

Vitelleschi, the sixth superior general, held the office for thirty years, from 1615 until 1645. Early in his generalate he presided over an extraordinarily happy occasion, the canonization in

1622 of Ignatius and Xavier, and over the great celebrations of the event throughout the Society. The celebration in the Roman College, though particularly splendid, is emblematic of others and, indeed, of the Jesuits' engagement with the arts to which their schools had committed them.

The entire inner space of the College was redesigned for the occasion for a celebration extending over several days. At one point a group of fifty-four students, wearing crowns, classical garb, and medals of Saint Ignatius, danced and sang a dithyramb, the lyrics of which could be read on a banner hanging on the walls. The central part of the celebration was entrusted to three theatrical performances, which succeeded one another in the ceremonial hall and required continual change in the enormous scenographic apparatus constructed for the occasion.

Theater had by then become a distinguishing mark of Jesuit schools and was considered by the Jesuits an essential component in their educational program. It taught poise and put eloquence, the mark of a leader in society, into practice. It sparked enthusiasm in the students and rescued them at least for a while from the drudgery of the classroom. Even schools of modest size generally produced two or three plays annually, which further anchored the institution as an essential element in the cultural life of the city. The limitations of "school drama" are well known, but to put it into perspective we need to recall that Lope de Vega, Calderón, Andreas Gryphius, Jacob Bidermann, Corneille, and Molière received their first training in theater in Jesuit schools.

Despite their concentration on literary genres as the core of the curriculum, many of the schools included a strong program in mathematics. Two years after the Roman College opened its doors, it added under the rubric of philosophy a chair of mathematics, understood to include geometry, optics, and astronomy. A major turning point occurred when in 1563 the German Jesuit Christoph Clavius assumed the chair, which he held until his death in 1612.

Clavius by force of his writings and the prestige he enjoyed among his peers launched a tradition that continued strong among the Jesuits until the suppression in 1773. An important consultant for Pope Gregory XIII on the reform of the calendar, he was also a teacher of Matteo Ricci, the Jesuit missionary in China, who used the mathematical skills he learned at the Roman College to win favor in the imperial court. Although Clavius had friendly relations with Galileo and supported some of his findings, he continued to hold to a basically Ptolemaic system.

The teaching of natural philosophy in Jesuit schools suffered from the condemnation of Galileo, but the discipline managed to survive and, though it for a while lagged behind in this rapidly developing field, it caught up. By the middle of the eighteenth century, physics taught in the Jesuits' colleges had largely assumed the characteristics of physics taught in other European schools. It by then was vastly different from what it had been when Clavius laid the groundwork. With the exception of Roger Boscovich (1711–1787), the Jesuits produced no scientist of first rank, but they kept abreast of what was going on and incorporated new developments into their teaching and writing.

Their vocation as missionaries provided them with opportunities for creating knowledge in geography, cartography, anthropology, and botany that were extraordinary. The reports the missionaries sent back became available to the larger academic community for two reasons special to the Jesuits. First, members of the Society were encouraged to keep up a steady correspondence among themselves. Second, what they wrote, especially about "curious" phenomena, was produced by men who were or had been teachers, and it got fed into a network of Jesuit teachers who knew how to exploit this information and release it into the public domain. In their classrooms all across Europe, for instance, Jesuits taught the geography they learned from the missionaries' maps.

José de Acosta's firsthand description of the lands and peoples of Peru and Mexico, *Historia natural y moral de las Indias*, is among the more important and famous of such Jesuit publications. First appearing in 1590, it within two decades went through four editions in Spanish, two in Dutch, two in French, three in Latin, two in German, and one in English. Meanwhile, dozens upon dozens of botanizing Jesuits described and gathered plant specimens from as far away as China, Ceylon (Sri Lanka), Paraguay, and Canada and sent them back home. This phenomenon enabled Jesuit teachers in Europe to assemble cabinets, create botanical gardens, and publish multivolume compendiums on natural history. The Jesuits opened pharmacies in which they distributed natural remedies such as quinine (known as "Jesuit bark") that their confreres had sent them from the missions.

The Jesuit educational and cultural enterprises display a coherence surprising for an organization made up of men from such different national and socioeconomic backgrounds stationed almost around the world. The coherence was due, most basically, to a shared European culture and then to Ignatius and his close collaborators, Polanco and Nadal, who produced a template of procedures that emphasized reflection, consultation, and clear articulation of goals and means. An outstanding product of that tradition relating to education is the *Ratio Studiorum* or "Plan of

Studies" issued in 1599 by Vitelleschi's predecessor as general, Claudio Aquaviva.

The *Ratio* was the result, typical of the Jesuits of this period, of widespread consultation and discussion within the Society. Its purpose was to ensure high standards and uniform practices in Jesuit schools in different parts of the world. In 1584 Aquaviva delegated a committee of six Jesuits to consolidate earlier documents addressing the subject. He then sent the results to the provinces for criticism, which poured into the Jesuit curia in Rome in great abundance. In 1591 he sent a new document for a three-year trial, which received a less negative response than the first. The results enabled him in 1599 to promulgate the definitive edition.

The *Ratio* consists essentially in a series of job descriptions for officials and teachers. It laid down the goals for each stage of the students' development and the pedagogical exercises that would ensure the goals were met. It reflected and codified assumptions about education common in the era, and therefore it assumed but did not articulate what those assumptions were. Only through inference can they be discovered. The *Ratio* without doubt stabilized practice in the Jesuit schools and set a high standard for them, which were huge benefits. But times change. The *Ratio* eventually began to impede the Jesuits' ability to respond to new circumstances, except when they decided virtually to ignore it or interpret it in the most generous way.

THE SOCIETY IN EUROPE

Jesuits exercised their ministries in many different countries and contexts. The history of the order, despite much that transcended specific situations, reflects this fact. In Italy during this period, for instance, they suffered only one major setback. When Pope Paul V in 1606 placed the Republic of Venice under interdict, the Jesuits, along with the Capuchins and Theatines, sided with the pope and were therefore expelled. Although the pope lifted the interdict the next year, the Republic did not readmit the Jesuits until fifty years later. The Society had already become identified as an agent of a foreign power, a problem that often made its situation precarious elsewhere as well.

In Italy the Jesuits otherwise enjoyed relative freedom and prosperity, largely due to the prestige that their schools brought them. The smashing success of the Roman College shed luster on all their educational institutions. The superiors general brought to its classrooms from everywhere in Europe the order's most gifted teachers, such as Clavius from Germany, Francisco Suárez from Spain, Pierre Perpinien from France, and Roberto Bellarmino from the Roman province itself.

Adding to the luster of that province and to Italy in general were two youths of noble blood who entered the Society and died young in Rome with a reputation for sanctity—the Pole Stanislaus Kostka and the Italian Aloysius Gonzaga. In 1605 Pope Paul V allowed them the title of "blessed," which was four years before he allowed the same for Ignatius. The Jesuits immediately held them up as models for the boys in their schools, and their portraits soon were to be found in every Jesuit church.

After the hostile pontificate of Paul IV, the popes generally took a favorable or neutral attitude toward the Society. Gregory XIII (1572–1585) was particularly friendly and showed special generosity toward the Roman College. Although Clement VIII (1592–1605) was not hostile to the Jesuits, he was certainly not particularly favorable. During his pontificate occurred the Society's first major internal crisis since the death of Ignatius. Its point of origin was Spain.

In a small but influential group of Spanish Jesuits, which included José de Acosta, smoldered resentment of Aquaviva for what they believed were his high-handed methods. But along with an animus against Aquaviva, they advocated that rectors and provincials be elected on the local level instead of being appointed by the general in Rome. Such a change in the *Constitutions* would be radical.

Through reports sent to Rome, these Jesuits aroused the concern, first, of Pope Sixtus V and then of his successor, Clement. Aquaviva was able to dissuade the former from taking action, but when the problem recurred under the latter, he was much less successful. Clement, conscientious but easily intimidated, ordered Aquaviva to convoke a General Congregation of the order, which perforce would be a challenge to Aquaviva personally but also to fundamental principles in the *Constitutions*. (In the Society a General Congregation was the equivalent of a General Chapter in other orders and had supreme authority in the Society.) Sixty-three delegates were duly elected in the Jesuit provinces around the world and came to Rome, where on November 3, 1593, they opened the Fifth General Congregation. The Congregation lasted two and half months. It overwhelmingly rejected the idea that the mode of governance stipulated in the *Constitutions* be changed in any way, and it rejected as unfounded the criticisms of Aquaviva. The critics had overplayed their hand. Their coup failed.

At just about the same time, both Aquaviva and Clement faced another problem that also arose in Spain. The Council of Trent in its Sixth Session, 1547, issued a long decree in response to Luther's teaching of "justification by faith alone." In its decree the council affirmed that both free will and grace were operative in the soul, but it did not try to explain just how that relationship worked, which left the question open to theologians. In 1588 the Spanish Jesuit Luis de Molina published his *Concordance of Free Will with the Gifts of Grace*, in which according to his major critic, Domingo Bañez, a distinguished Dominican theologian, he attributed so much to free will as to fall into the heresy known as Pelagianism.

A major battle broke out. All at once the Spanish Jesuits and the Spanish Dominicans seemed to be fighting a contest unto death, in which the Jesuits accused the Dominicans of being Calvinists, and the Dominicans accused the Jesuits of being Pelagians. The controversy escalated to such a degree that in 1594 Pope Clement ordered the affair be brought to Rome for adjudication. There for more than ten years the debate raged, with Clement reaching no decision. Finally in 1607 the new pope, Paul V, ordered a cease-fire and forbade both the Jesuits and Dominicans from ever denouncing the doctrine of the other as dangerous or heretical. For the Jesuits the controversy brought to the surface and helped crystallize a bias toward free agency that became typical of them.

These two problems that arose in Spain while Aquaviva was general obscure how well the Society was prospering there. The schools enjoyed great prestige, Jesuit confessors were sought after by high and low, and Jesuit preachers drew large crowds. The colleges and residences became hubs from which during vacation periods teams of Jesuits radiated to the countryside, moving from hamlet to hamlet among the humblest strata of society in intensive programs in preaching, teaching catechism, and working to quell vendettas.

In central Europe, the Jesuits of the German assistancy profited from the leadership that Peter Canisius provided for almost a half century. Like much of the rest of the Society, they continued to grow in numbers and public esteem. They without doubt were Catholicism's strongest bulwark against the Reformation and were uncompromising in their opposition to it. In Protestant eyes the Jesuits became the very embodiment of the dreaded Counter-Reformation.

In the early seventeenth century, the political and religious situation took an especially ugly and destructive turn with the outbreak of the Thirty Years War, 1618–1648. Originally a contest between Catholic and Lutheran forces "in German lands," it escalated to an international power struggle. On one side stood Catholic Austria, Bavaria, and Spain, and on the other Catholic France. The battles were fought almost exclusively on German soil and left many areas utterly devastated.

Vitelleschi's thirty-year tenure as general, 1615–1645, corresponded almost precisely with the dates of the war. Among the other problems he faced because of the war was that Jesuits were the confessors of the monarchs of all four of the great Catholic powers. He again and again forbade them to use their role in any way to influence political policy, but that was a distinction more easily drawn in theory than in practice. Wilhelm Lamormaini became Emperor Ferdinand II's confessor in 1624 and worked to convince him that his destiny was the restoration of Catholicism in all the Habsburg lands.

During his time as Ferdinand's confessor, Lamormaini had a particularly high profile and soon became regarded, with considerable justification, as the power behind the throne. His opposition to any compromise with Protestants won him enemies near and far, and it resulted in a sharp rise in anti-Jesuit feeling even among

Catholics. Vitelleschi felt helpless as long as Lamormaini enjoyed the emperor's favor. The notoriety surrounding Lamormaini and the well-known fact that Jesuits were confessors to other monarchs gained for them the reputation of political meddlers and international schemers.

In 1614, just before the Thirty Years War began, the anonymous and scurrilous *Monita Secreta* appeared in Kraków to become almost immediately one of the most influential sources of the "black legend" about the Jesuits. It was a small book that had a big impact and was published and republished in all the major vernaculars into the twentieth century. A crude forgery, it purported to be secret instructions from the superior general of the Society telling select members how to fleece widows of their fortunes, how to use confessional secrets to blackmail rulers, and how by these and other despicable means to climb to the pinnacle of political power. Refuted and denounced as soon as published, no other book, except possibly Pascal's *Provincial Letters*, so effectively poisoned opinion against the Jesuits.

At about the same time in Poland, where Calvinism had won the minds and hearts of the nobility, the Jesuits found support for their efforts in King Sigismund III, who reigned in the crucial years 1587–1632. The alliance of the Jesuits with the monarchy won them enemies among the nobility and helped foster an atmosphere where the *Monita* seemed credible. Important though royal support was, the Jesuits could not have been as well received as they generally were had it not been for their own merits. The schools, attended by many students whose parents were not Catholic, were, again, a crucial factor. In 1626 there were twenty-eight in the vast Polish-Lithuanian Commonwealth.

But the schools are not the whole story. The Jesuits found a particularly warm response to their preaching. To listen to a Jesuit sermon became a fashionable pastime even for Protestants. Careful to master the Ruthenian and Lithuanian languages, the preachers by constant use helped keep these tongues alive. Piotr Skarga's *Lives of the Saints*, 1579, and Jakub Wujek's elegant translation of the Bible, 1599, were widely read and contributed to the development of the Polish language. In time the Jesuits were accepted, therefore, as true Poles.

However, the suspicion that the Jesuits were foreigners dogged them in France almost from the beginning and added to the difficulties that the Faculty of Theology's condemnation in 1554 continued to cause them. The Jesuits did their best to carry on as they did elsewhere, despite the immense problems thrust upon them with the outbreak in 1562 of almost thirty years of religious conflict between Catholics and Huguenots that tore the country apart. Even in this difficult situation, there were in 1575 more than three hundred men divided into two provinces, and by 1580 they were conducting fifteen colleges.

In contrast to the welcome Jesuits received in some parts of the country, in Paris the university and Parlement kept up a barrage of accusations and denunciation. The Jesuits, supported by the crown, got caught in the cross fire between the monarchy and its enemies. Matters only got worse. The assassination of King Henry III in 1589 brought to the throne the Huguenot Henry of Navarre. Although Navarre converted to Catholicism, the Jesuits were forbidden by Aquaviva to take the required oath of loyalty until the papacy lifted Henry's excommunication. The Jesuits' abstention from the oath put them in a compromised position and added to the persuasion that they were not true Frenchmen.

Then an event took place that brought their situation to full crisis. An emotionally disturbed young man, a former student at the Jesuits' Collège de Clermont, made an attempt on Henry IV's life. His connection with the Jesuits, tenuous though it was, gave the Society's enemies the excuse they needed to expel it from Paris and environs. On September 17, 1595, Clement gave absolution to Henry, and a year and a half later requested that the Jesuits be readmitted to the capital. The king was gradually won over and in fact became a friend of the Society. On September 1, 1603, he issued the Edict of Rouen, formally reestablishing it in France.

The edict's importance can be gauged from the fact that within five months of its publication, thirty-two towns requested Jesuit colleges. From the thirty-two the king chose eighteen and made his favorite the one he started at La Flèche, near Angers. Converting the graceful and elegant Châteauneuf into the school, he envisaged it as "the most beautiful in the world," and the Collège Royal Henry-Le Grand at La Flèche did indeed become one of the most esteemed and prestigious of the Jesuit schools in the whole Jesuit network. René Descartes entered La Flèche at the age of eight as one of its first students and remained for twelve years. It was the only formal schooling he ever had.

For the moment, therefore, all seemed well for the Jesuits in France. A strong and enduring bond had been formed between them and the crown, which guaranteed them royal favor. But such favor was not without its liabilities, as events would show.

In perhaps no other territory did the Society prosper as much in the late sixteenth and seventeenth centuries as in Belgium. By 1592 the Jesuits already ran eleven colleges there and were engaged in a massive program of catechizing that reached deep into the population. They formed a close and cordial relationship with the community of artisans and artists that soon produced works of art that the Jesuits distributed in every part of the world, most especially to the missions overseas. They were especially close to Peter Paul Rubens, who decorated for them the interior of their great church in Antwerp, the first in the world dedicated to Saint Ignatius. They produced a Jesuit artist of distinction, Daniël Seghers (1590–1661). In 1612 Aquaviva divided Belgium into two provinces according to language and pronounced it "the flower of the Society of Jesus."

The Jesuits were compulsive record keepers, as demonstrated by the figures the Flemish Jesuits made public about their ministries in the single year 1640. They and their lay helpers, for instance, taught catechism 10,045 times to 32,508 children and adults. The province had ninety Marian congregations with almost 14,000 members. Antwerp alone had ten with some 3,000 members, which included Rubens. The Professed House in Antwerp provided twenty-six confessors on call for the adjacent church, where within the space of a year Jesuits administered communion 240,000 times. In Brussels over the course of fifteen years, the Jesuits gave spiritual comfort to 344 men as they prepared for their execution. Although Belgium itself had no overseas missions, the Jesuits there claimed a share in the merits of the English and Scots martyrs—Edmund Campion, Robert Southwell, John Ogilvie, and others—because their schools educated these (and many other) English recusants.

In 1580 three English Jesuits—Campion, Robert Persons, and Ralph Emerson—entered England in disguise. They eventually were joined by others, but even by 1610 the number had grown to only fifty-two. Their situation, always difficult and dangerous,

worsened considerably in 1605 when they were suspected of col-
lusion in the Gunpowder Plot to assassinate King James I. The
"English mission" of the Jesuits ran into ever more difficulties,
including opposition from other priests. Somehow it managed to
continue and in an utterly unexpected turn of events to father a
mission of great importance for the future of Catholicism.

George Calvert, first Baron of Baltimore, converted to
Catholicism, at least partly due to the ministrations of the Jesuit
Andrew White. His son Leonard wanted to colonize lands held by
the family in the area of the Chesapeake Bay in North America.
In so doing he also wanted to provide a refuge for Catholics where
they might worship freely. He enlisted Andrew White and two
other Jesuits to accompany the expedition, which was made up of
both Catholics and Anglicans. On March 25, 1634, the colonists
arrived on St. Clement's Island in what was to become, first, the
English colony of Maryland and then, after the American Revolution, one of the original thirteen states in the new United States.

Although the colony was founded on a principle of religious
toleration, waves of bitter anti-Catholicism periodically broke out.
Still, some Catholic families prospered and were regarded with
respect and deference. The Jesuits, the only Catholic priests in the
colony, continued to grow by small increments through entry into
the Society of young men from Maryland itself. They worked to
convert the ever diminishing number of aborigines and to minister
to the relatively small Catholic population, which they did by pro-
viding them with mass, the sacraments, and basic catechesis. Compared to other overseas undertakings by the Society, Maryland was
among the least venturesome and the least promising for the
future.

THE SOCIETY OVERSEAS

Ever since the late fifteenth century, Dominicans, Franciscans, and Augustinians had sailed with the galleons of Portugal and Spain as they set out to explore and exploit "the Indies," the generic term of the era to indicate Asia and the Americas. The Jesuits came late on the scene but soon began to play an important and in some places a dominant role. Despite their massive commitment to the ministry of formal schooling, they never forgot that they were founded as a missionary order and that their professed members pronounced a special (Fourth) vow "concerning missions."

By the time Ignatius died in 1556, Jesuits had not only set foot in India, Japan, and Brazil but also in the Congo and were on their way to Ethiopia. The moving force behind these ventures was King John III of Portugal, and it was under his aegis and in his domains that the Jesuits first made their mark as missionaries. In Africa the Jesuits became engaged in five large areas: Ethiopia, Mozambique, Angola, the Congo, and Cape Verde. Although from the days of Saint Ignatius himself, Jesuit hopes were high for bringing the Coptic church in Ethiopia into the Roman fold, they despite repeated efforts over a long period made little headway. In the other areas of Africa the missions stalled especially because of lack of manpower but also because the Jesuits were so ill informed about the situations they met and therefore were ill prepared to deal with them effectively. Moreover, they sometimes made the fatal mistake of identifying themselves too closely with the Portuguese military.

The situation was very different in the Far East. When Xavier took leave of King John III on April 7, 1541, to begin his long voyage to India, he had in hand four papal briefs from Pope Paul

III appointing him papal nuncio in the Indies and recommending him to the princes ruling in the East. Thirteen months later he arrived in Goa, the capital of Portuguese India, which would become the first headquarters for Jesuit missionary activity in that part of the world.

Xavier remained in Goa only four months, then worked for two years among the poor pearl fishers on the eastern side of Cape Comorin (Kanyakumari), the southern extremity of India. After that he traveled to the outmost bounds of Portuguese influence in the Far East, present-day Indonesia, four thousand miles beyond India. He returned to Goa to organize the mission. At that time there were about thirty Jesuits in India, but within five years another twenty-five had arrived. The Jesuits divided their labors between working for the conversion of the native population and ministering to the relatively large Portuguese population in those parts. The Jesuits blamed the greed and bad example of the Portuguese for their failure to make many converts.

The Jesuits' most exotic venture in India was the mission to the court of the Great Mughal, the emperors Akbar (1556–1605) and Jahangir (1605–1627). Northern India was at the time enjoying a climate of remarkable creativity and cultural openness. Its worldly rulers invited scholars, priests, and other holy men from around the world to their courts, where they engaged them in weekly interfaith debates into the small hours of the morning. The emperors and their guests expounded on the texts and traditions of faiths as varied as Islam, Hinduism, and Zoroastrianism.

Akbar, a man of insatiable intellectual curiosity and, though professedly a Muslim, an eclectic in religion, in 1578 requested "two learned priests" to come from Goa to Fatehpur to serve as representatives there of Catholicism. In 1580 three Jesuits arrived led by Rodolfo Aquaviva, whose uncle Claudio would be elected superior general the next year. At the insistence of Akbar, they plunged immediately into the debates over which he presided. They soon came to realize that, though the Great Mughal treated them with respect and kindness, they were for him more a source to satisfy his curiosity than serious contenders for his religious allegiance.

Nonetheless, the Jesuits founded a permanent mission there in 1598 and remained, with a few interruptions, until the suppression of 1773. They served the emperors well, bringing with them to northern India engravings, printed books, and oil paintings. Akbar himself was fascinated by Christian altarpieces and by the way the Jesuits used taffeta curtains, incense, and candles to enhance the spiritual power of their images. The urbanity of the Mughal court contrasted with the hostility the Jesuits faced elsewhere, due in large part to their being identified in the popular mind with the hated Portuguese.

In 1570 the mission to Brazil suffered a tragic loss of life. In that year, forty Jesuits set out for Brazil under the leadership of Ignacio de Azevedo. They were intercepted on the high seas by the Huguenot corsair Jacques Sourie. When Sourie discovered who the Jesuits were, he ordered them executed and their bodies cast into the sea. Back in Catholic Europe, they were immediately celebrated as saints, and they were in fact beatified in 1854.

Despite this loss of reinforcements, the mission to Brazil continued to prosper as it had from the beginning. Its prosperity was due to a number of factors but not least to the marvelous leadership provided early on by Nóbrega and Anchieta. The broad scope of Jesuit action in Brazil was twofold: the seacoast towns and the deep forests. In the towns the colleges, directed to the Portuguese and Creole population, were here as elsewhere the center of Jesuit operations. They soon became mature institutions. When in 1566 the Portuguese wrested Rio de Janeiro from the French, Nóbrega transferred Jesuit headquarters there, where he soon opened a novitiate and a house of studies for the training of Jesuit scholastics. At Bahia in 1572, the college introduced philosophy into its curriculum and a few years later conferred its first master's degrees. Firm foundations for the future were thus laid.

Among the Indians, the Jesuit objective was to settle them in fixed communities, known as *aldeias*, where they could be weaned from superstition, drunkenness, and cannibalism and be instructed in the Christian faith. When Anchieta was involved in the process, it went reasonably well through his amazing output of lively and attractive songs, hymns, and religious plays. Even as Anchieta was molding the spiritual temper of early Brazil, he was laying the foundations for a national culture.

Although such efforts smack of paternalism and were inspired by a sense of cultural superiority, they were not engaged in by the Jesuits without some feeling of mutuality, and they contrast favorably with the attitudes and practices of many other Europeans who had settled there. In Brazil Jesuits took courageous stands against the enslavement of the natives and evoked great wonderment as word sped through the jungles that among the Portuguese there were some who defended them.

Although the Jesuits arrived in Brazil in 1549, they did not enter the Spanish domains of the western hemisphere until nineteen years later, 1568. The delay was due to the wary attitude toward the Society of Philip II. Unlike in Brazil, where the Jesuits were the first missionaries to arrive, the Dominicans, Franciscans, and other orders had arrived in Spanish territories some seventy-five years before they did and were well established. This situation brought the Jesuits the advantage of being able to learn from the experience of the others but the disadvantage of being drawn into the sometimes unseemly, even vicious, competition among religious orders.

Once arrived the Jesuits soon entered three major areas claimed by the Spanish crown—Florida, Mexico, and Peru. In the first they suffered incredible hardships, made no headway with the Indians, and met death at their hands. The survivors retreated either to Havana, where they and their confreres soon opened a college, or to Mexico City to begin another successful chapter in the Society's history. In Mexico by 1574 the Jesuits had, with their church and school for six hundred boys in Mexico City and their schools at Oaxaca and Patzcuaro, entered as an important force into the cultural and religious life of the colony.

Among the first to arrive in the Viceroy of Peru was Alonso Barzana, who penetrated into the wilds of upper Peru and then into the eastern valleys of the Andes. These experiences allowed him to produce a dictionary and a prayer book in five Indian dialects. He was not alone among the Jesuits in his mastery of such languages and dialects. But the most enduring of the Jesuit undertakings in these early years was the founding of the college of San Pablo in Lima almost as soon as they arrived in the Viceroy. The oldest Jesuit school in Spanish America, San Pablo developed into a nerve center in the New World for the entry of European intellectual currents, and for two centuries it sparked the cultural life of Peru.

With the native populations in the forests of this vast territory, the Jesuits for the most part met hostility, identified as they perforce were with the Spanish aggressors. However, the mission among the more peaceful Guaraní was an exception, and it was among them that the Jesuits developed the famous reductions, permanent settlements that were meant to protect the Indians from slave traders, teach them skills so that they might support themselves and pay the onerous taxes imposed by the government, and, finally, provide an atmosphere conducive to the practice of Catholicism.

Although Madrid set down the firm policy that none but Spaniards emigrate to "the Spanish Indies," the Jesuits somehow circumvented it. Their work there almost from the beginning had a remarkably international character, reflective of the international character of the Society of Jesus itself. Of those sent to Mexico, for example, between about 1575 and 1625, thirty-seven of the Jesuits came from Italy, seventeen from Portugal, seven from France, five from the Low Countries, and others from other places, including Denmark and Ireland. In the latter part of the seventeenth century, the influx of German Jesuits especially in the Viceroy of Peru was considerable.

Regarding international staffing, the Portuguese were more tolerant than the Spaniards. The crown had no problem, for instance, that Xavier, a Spaniard, was the first priest to open the mission to Japan, where he arrived on August 15, 1549, accompanied by Father Cosmé de Torres, Brother Juan Fernández, and a Japanese recently converted to Catholicism named Paul of the Holy Faith. After several ill-advised ventures in trying to reach persons of authority who might help him, Xavier approached Ouchi Yoshitaka, daimyo of Yamagochi, a prince of real power, who, Xavier immediately realized, would be impressed only with a display of grandeur.

Xavier abandoned the simple clerical attire he had worn elsewhere and appeared in court finely robed. He presented his credentials as an ambassador of Portugal and gave Yoshitaka an elaborate assortment of gifts, including a clock, eyeglasses, a music box, wine, and more still. The daimyo, fascinated and delighted with the gifts, gave Xavier permission to preach and also put an unused Buddhist temple at his disposal.

With that incident the Japanese mission got under way and did so with considerable success almost from that moment. Official approval of these visitors from a strange land made the difference. Xavier was deeply and favorably impressed with the Japanese. He wrote back to Goa that the Japanese "are the finest yet discovered. . . . They are good and not malicious, with a marvelous sense of honor and esteem for it."[1] Xavier's assessment was shared by others and made the Japanese mission attractive to members of the Society. Within thirty years, some sixty Jesuits were active there, an unmistakable sign of a successful venture. An even more unmistakable sign was the thousands of converts the Jesuits won.

In 1579 the young, talented, and decisive Italian Jesuit Alessandro Valignano arrived, armed by the superior general with the official title of Visitor, which gave him almost plenipotentiary powers. As he assessed the situation in Japan, he too was struck by the high level of Japanese culture and the need for a policy that took it into account. He determined that the missionaries abandon European dress, diet, and customs so as to conform themselves as far as possible with the culture of Japan. He opened a novitiate for the training of Japanese recruits to the Society, for he saw that the future of Christianity in Japan rested with a native clergy. In 1602 two Japanese Jesuits were ordained priests. More followed.

The most visible and physical evidence of the degree to which the Jesuits tried to adapt to their new land was the way they built their churches, which were utterly different from any style prevailing in Europe. They adopted many features of Buddhist temples and built in the Japanese style of post-and-lintel wooden architecture, with hipped-gable roofs. Rather than a single freestanding building, the church proper formed part of a complex that might contain ablution fountains, fishponds, and gardens.

At the instigation of Valignano, the Italian Jesuit Giovanni Niccolò in 1583 founded an art school and studio that had an extraordinary impact on Japanese art outside the mission community. The school grew over the course of the years, and by the end of the century may have employed as many as forty artists. Students painted in oil on copper and wood and occasionally on canvas. They also executed paintings in Japanese watercolors. The school had a foundry, where small statues were cast. The school also made bells, clocks, and musical instruments.

The mission thrived. By the early seventeenth century, there were some three hundred thousand Catholic Christians in Japan. Under the surface, however, serious problems smoldered, including an ever shifting political situation that was closely related to Japanese reactions to Portuguese traders and trade policies. Fear grew that the missionaries might be acting as a fifth column to prepare for a Spanish invasion of Japan launched from the Philippines.

The first blow fell on February 5, 1597, when twenty-six Christians, including three Japanese Jesuits, were crucified at Nagasaki. The fatal blow fell on January 27, 1614, when all missionaries were expelled from Japan and all Japanese Christians ordered to return to the practice of Buddhism. The decree ended the mission, where by that time 116 Jesuits labored, who with their lay catechists and other helpers made up a staff of more than 500 persons. Christianity would not return to Japan until the middle of the nineteenth century.

Ever since Xavier, Jesuits dreamed of entering China. It was Valignano, convinced the Jesuits had to dissociate themselves from the image of the westerner as marauder, who finally made the venture possible by the same program of enculturation he developed for Japan. He assigned two brilliant young Italians—Michele Ruggieri and Matteo Ricci—to the task of learning Chinese. Ready by 1583, the two gained entrance into the kingdom and eventually made their way to the capital, Beijing.

Ricci, by virtue of his marvelous gifts of mind and heart, his scientific skills, and his command of the language and the classics of Chinese literature, was able by 1594 to win the emperor's favor and enter the elite social class of the mandarins, whose style of dress he adopted. He sought ways to show the compatibility of Confucianism with Christianity, much the way Aquinas and others earlier tried to show Aristotle's compatibility. Unlike the Greeks with Aristotle, however, the Chinese honored Confucius in ritual ways. Ricci maintained that these rites were devoid of religious significance. But that was a position difficult to prove, and it became the center point of a controversy that ultimately proved disastrous.

Nonetheless, in these early years the mission in Beijing gave great promise. When Ricci died in 1610, there were some four hundred Catholics in the capital and many thousands in other parts of the country where Jesuits labored using more traditional approaches. Disappointing to Ricci and his successors was the minuscule number of conversions among the learned, who were ready to learn what the "western barbarians" had to teach them but felt no inclination to embrace their religion.

In succeeding decades political upheavals made the Jesuits' position difficult, and for five years they had to go into hiding.

The Jesuits persevered, however, and in 1618 twenty-two new missionaries set sail from Lisbon with China as their destination. Among them was the brilliant German astronomer Johann Adam Schall von Bell and the Swiss astronomer Johann Terrenz Schreck, who brought with him a science library of about seven thousand volumes. Although the Jesuits' position was often precarious, the learning of men like Schall and Schreck won respect and helped stave off the more drastic measures that might have been taken against them.

In India the Italian nobleman Roberto De Nobili (1577–1656) reached the city of Madurai in South India in 1606, and for most of the next forty years worked as a missionary there. Dismayed at the policy of forcing Portuguese names and customs upon converts, he decided to adopt the dress, customs, diet, and manner of life of the Hindu holy man. He was one of the first Europeans to learn Tamil and perhaps the first to write a theological treatise in that or any Indian language. His life was dedicated to the proposition that to become a Christian one did not have to become a European. He and his Jesuit successors, especially the Portuguese nobleman João de Brito (1647–1693), had limited success, due in part to their small numbers, but they were the pioneers that later generations emulated.

The Catholic mission in the East that had the most lasting success by far was the mission to the Philippines, which resulted in the only country in that part of the world with a population overwhelmingly Catholic. In 1581 Antonio Sedeño, who nine years earlier had founded the mission to Mexico, arrived in Manila with three other Jesuits. Within a decade some hundred Jesuits were working in several of the islands, cooperating with and competing with other orders that had arrived earlier. Through the seventeenth century, the number of men in the province hovered between about 100 and 130. Although the Jesuits made important contributions to the Philippine mission, they share the success with the other orders.

France was late in trying to establish an overseas empire, but in 1608 Samuel de Champlain founded Quebec City and thus New France. A small group of Jesuits led by Paul Le Jeune arrived in 1632 and within three years had founded in Quebec City the College of Our Lady of the Angels. The harshness of the climate, the indifference or hostility of the native peoples, and the primitive character of life even in the French settlements made this an especially difficult mission, and the Jesuits suffered terribly.

Posthumous portrait of Ignatius of Loyola by Jacopino del Conte, 1556. Courtesy of the Curia Generalizia of the Society of Jesus, Rome.

Detail of the collegiate church of Saints Peter and Paul in Krakow. The facade is one of the most dramatic examples of the international influence of the Jesuits' mother church, the Gesù in Rome.

Statue of Saint Francis Xavier in Goa, India.

Facade of Saint Paul's church in Macau, which was the
administrative center for Jesuit ministry in Southeast Asia.
Today the facade is a UNESCO World Heritage Site.

Interior of the Church of the Society of Jesus in Cusco, Peru.

São Miguel das Missões was one of the many Jesuit reductions in South America. It is now a UNESCO World Heritage Site.

Jesuit college at Orsha (Orsza), Belarus

*Statue of Matteo Ricci at Saint Paul's church in Macau,
where Ricci studied Chinese. Courtesy of Rev. Ronald Anton, SJ*

Catherine the Great refused to suppress the Jesuits and played a vital role in maintaining their training.

Healy Hall at Georgetown University. Courtesy of Georgetown University.

Pedro Arrupe, SJ, the twenty-eighth
superior general of the Society of
Jesus. Courtesy of the Curia Generalizia
of the Society of Jesus, Rome.

3

CONSOLIDATION, CONTROVERSY, CALAMITY

Reassured by the celebrations of their first century, the Jesuits moved with confidence into their second. Although the Japanese mission, a venture of which they had been particularly proud, ended in tragedy, that failure was an exception. In virtually every other place where they had established themselves, they seemed to move ever more deeply into the religious and cultural fabric and to give it characteristics distinctive of themselves. They consolidated and further developed enterprises earlier undertaken.

Perhaps no more graphic illustration of this phenomenon can be found than in the elaborate network of reciprocally supportive institutions that the Jesuits constructed in Spanish America. The network integrated their urban and rural enterprises into a system in which, though each enterprise stood on its own, it also provided benefits to the others. In the cities the Jesuits opened schools and constructed impressive churches. But their urban holdings extended much further and included hospitals, pharmacies, and retreat houses. In major cities such as Cusco or La Paz, they ran *tambos*, which were guesthouses or modest hotels where travelers might stay.

The larger schools, moreover, contained printing presses and housed extensive libraries with books published locally but also books imported from Europe on almost every imaginable subject. Some also operated astronomical observatories. The most celebrated school, San Ildefonso in Mexico City, whose construction was completed in the middle of the eighteenth century, was favorably compared with the schools of Spain, Italy, and France, but other schools in Spanish America equaled or almost equaled that standard of excellence. As in Europe, the schools became the major agent in mounting on a sometimes grandiose scale religious and civic celebrations, in which every stratum of society played a role. By the middle of the eighteenth century, the Jesuits in the northern region of Spanish America—Mexico, Guatemala, and Cuba—were stationed in 40 colleges and residences and in 114 missions. Staffing these establishments were about 680 Jesuits.

Ongoing financing of the schools was a problem here as elsewhere. The rents and products from the Jesuits' holdings in the countryside were enlisted and organized to offset school costs. The Jesuits operated ranches, plantations, and fulling mills in which agricultural activity and the raising of livestock were often combined with an industry, such as sugar production and cloth making. For such institutions to function, waterworks were required to provide for drinking, washing, and manufacturing as well as for the movement of goods, which meant the construction of canals, dikes, dams, and mills. Some missions operated by the Jesuits contained potteries and silversmitheries, and others produced high-quality religious images and musical instruments, including organs.

The reductions, self-sufficient and self-governing communities of Amerindians, are of course the best known of the Jesuit enterprises in Latin America. Although the two or three Jesuits residing in them had the final word, the immediate authority for governance belonged to a council of the natives that possessed legislative, executive, and judicial power over perhaps as many as ten thousand inhabitants of a given reduction. These were not small settlements!

Each reduction contained flour mills, bakeries, slaughterhouses, and similar institutions, with an ample water supply and a sophisticated sewer system. The church, the most impressive building in a reduction, was the site of elaborate liturgies. At their peak, toward the middle of the eighteenth century, the urban development of the reductions equaled or surpassed that of neighboring cities, with the exception of Buenos Aires and Córdoba. The heaviest penalty for anyone convicted of criminal activity was ten years' imprisonment. The death penalty did not exist, which was unique for the era.

In China the Jesuits attained the height of their success during the reign of Emperor Kangxi (reign 1661–1722), the longest rule in Chinese history. Highly intelligent and inquisitive, Kangxi was attracted to his Jesuit courtiers for their knowledge and personal gifts. In his youth the Jesuits acted as his tutors and later served him in several important instances, which included helping him quell a major rebellion and facilitating for him his relationship with western powers. In gratitude for these and other services, Kangxi issued in 1692 an edict of toleration of Christians, which inaugurated the most promising dozen or so years in the entire history of the mission. The edict and the excellent relations between the emperor and the Jesuits led Louis Le Comte (1655–1728), a

French Jesuit returned to France from China, to publish a eulogistic biography of Kangxi as an extraordinarily wise and prudent ruler, a philosopher-king.

The French Jesuit missionaries convinced the emperor of the usefulness of a full-scale map of his domains. Kangxi undertook the project and, with the Jesuit cartographers and a large entourage, traveled to different parts of his empire to oversee it. The project turned out to be the largest cartographic endeavor based on exact measurements ever undertaken anywhere in the world. Similar projects in France and Russia, for instance, were not completed until decades later. In the project's final stages, the French Jesuit Pierre Jartoux (1669–1720) led efforts to combine regional maps to produce a large overview that enabled the emperor to take in his vast empire in a single glance.

In Europe the Jesuits continued to draw large congregations to their churches, continued in many places to send their teams of missionaries to villages in the hinterlands, and continued as chaplains in prisons and hospitals. Their Marian congregations flourished, and especially in Naples, probably the most musically alive city in Europe at the time, they sponsored well-attended concerts of sacred music in the great Jesuit church, the Gesù Nuovo. In 1722 the Marian congregation attached to the Jesuit church of San Fedele in Milan sponsored there the premiere of Vivaldi's last oratorio, *The Adoration of the Magi*.

The colleges, despite significant challenges from a changing culture, sometimes a crushing debt, and, now, competition from the schools of other religious orders, continued to enjoy great prestige and play an important cultural role in the cities and towns where they were located. They were civic institutions of the first order, founded for the good of the city and often in some form funded by the city. In this age before public libraries, the library in the Jesuit school was generally the largest and most important in the city, and the entertainment offered by the plays the school produced was sometimes the best available, especially in smaller towns. As late as 1741, for instance, the city of Milan called upon the Jesuits to orchestrate the elaborate program of public mourning for the death of Emperor Charles VI.

The College of Nobles founded in Milan in 1682 soon had an outstanding reputation. The curriculum was up to date and taught by celebrated teachers, including the famous scientist Roger Boscovich. Besides Latin, the three hundred or so students learned French and German, and they studied astronomy, mathematics, physics, history, geography, and hydrography. The repertoire of the college theater included a few comedies inspired by Molière and a tragedy derived from Corneille. Racine's *Athalie* served as a model for tragedies about biblical figures written by the Jesuits and performed by the students. But Milan was not unique. In Paris the Collège Louis-le-Grand had an outstanding faculty of Jesuit teachers and writers that drew a correspondingly brilliant body of students—including Voltaire!

As baroque culture developed, the Society became ever more identified with some of its leading artists. Gian Lorenzo Bernini, a friend of the superior general, Gian Paolo Oliva, designed for the Jesuits the new church in Rome of Sant'Andrea al Quirinale, completed in 1671, one of the gems of baroque architecture. Oliva at the urging of Bernini meanwhile engaged Giovani Battista Gaulli (known as "Baciccio") to decorate the interior of the Jesuits' mother church, the Gesù, and give it the form it retains to this day.

Oliva brought to Rome Brother Andrea Pozzo, who among his many other works decorated the interior of the church of San Ignazio, the church attached to the Roman College and built to commemorate the canonization of Ignatius. Pozzo later went on to a brilliant career. In 1693–1698 he published in two volumes in Latin and Italian one of the era's most important works on perspective, soon translated into every major European language as well as into Chinese. Sir Christopher Wren wrote a preface for the English translation in 1707. After working extensively in Rome and elsewhere in Italy, Pozzo died in 1709 in Vienna, where he had been summoned in 1702 by Emperor Leopold I.

Other Jesuit artists produced works of high quality. Much earlier in Cusco and elsewhere in Spanish America, Brother Bernado Bitti's slender mannerist figures were highly prized. From Chile in the early eighteenth century, the accomplished sculptor Johann Bitterich asked his Jesuit superiors in Europe to send him artists and craftsmen. In 1724 fifteen architects, woodcarvers, pewterers, smelters, silversmiths, and weavers arrived, all Jesuits. In 1747 another twenty-three came, bringing with them 386 crates of materials and tools, and seven years later came a dozen more.

In the eighteenth century under the Qing dynasty, the most important period of Jesuit artistic activity in China took place, at the center of which was Giuseppe Castiglione (1688–1766), known as Shining Lang. Besides an extraordinary number of paintings, designs for engravings, architectural plans, and the translation into Chinese of Pozzo's treatise on perspective, he planned the palace pavilions at the emperor's summer residence near Beijing. Castiglione served his imperial masters for an astounding fifty-one years and taught Chinese artists techniques of European oil painting.

During this century, therefore, there is considerable evidence of vibrancy and of effective engagement with cultural and religious issues. But it was a long century. As it moved along, more and more problems emerged for the Society, and as hindsight makes clear, they began to coalesce so as to threaten the Jesuits' very survival. Some were internal to the Society. Among them, for instance, was how to sustain an austere personal life in institutions of ever greater sophistication. By and large it seems the Jesuits handled this problem reasonably well, despite the image of wealth some of their institutions projected.

Although membership in the Society continued to grow, it was at a slower pace, and in given areas the pattern fluctuated considerably. In some provinces, for instance, it moved from steady increase, to alarming slump, followed sometimes by at least partial recuperation. The slump sometimes occurred simply because the province did not have enough money to support the novices. The situation became so severe that in 1645 the Eighth General Congregation instructed the new superior general, Vincenzo Carafa, to limit the number of novices provinces might accept depending on their ability to support them, and even, if necessary, to prohibit provinces from accepting any at all.

War, plague, and rapidly shifting political regimes also took their toll. But the picture is mixed. By 1710 the numbers in the Gallo-Belgian province had dropped some 40 percent from what they were a century earlier. At roughly the same time, however, the German provinces continued to grow, and by 1773 the Austrian province had expanded to include some 1,800 members, one of the largest memberships in the entire history of the Society.

In fact, by 1750 membership in the Society worldwide reached a peak for the pre-suppression era, in contrast with the

Dominicans, whose membership had begun to decline. Jesuits numbered about 22,500, just slightly fewer than the Dominicans. The membership in these two orders combined did not, however, come close to equaling the number of men following the Rule of Saint Francis in the three branches of that order. In 1750 their number exceeded a hundred and forty thousand.

Although the schools seemed to be flourishing, they had to deal with two new challenges to the very foundations of their program. The first was the attack on the assumption that the classics of Greece and Rome were "the best" literature and alone to be taught in the schools. This "quarrel of the Ancients and the Moderns" had long been simmering, but it became serious in the last decades of the seventeenth century. By then the brilliance of the "moderns" had become ever more evident in authors such as Tasso, Cervantes, Montaigne, Molière, and Shakespeare, to say nothing of older authors such as Dante and Boccaccio.

Moreover, French had replaced Latin as the international language of diplomacy and of intellectual and literary communication. The ability to speak and write in Latin lost practical appeal except for clerics. Although the Jesuit schools had consistently cultivated vernacular eloquence as well as Latin, the *Ratio* had set the classical curriculum in stone and made it difficult for the Jesuits to respond in a systemic way to this cultural shift. Other orders now engaged in formal schooling for boys were able to be more flexible.

The second challenge resulted from the impact of Galileo and especially the publication in 1687 of Newton's *Principia Mathematica*, which along with other works of the era discredited the Aristotelian basis of science. As mentioned, the Jesuits strove to keep abreast and were recognized as doing so. In 1685, for instance, six French Jesuits set sail from Brest for Siam. They traveled as *Mathématiciens du Roi*

(Louis XIV) and carried with them telescopes, quadrants, seconds-pendulum, and other instruments to measure longitude by observing the satellites of Jupiter during an eclipse. Their project was sponsored not by the Society of Jesus but by the Paris Académie Royale des Sciences, an unmistakable sign of the esteem in which the Jesuits were held in the secular world.

But as late as 1730 the Sixteenth General Congregation and then again in 1751 the next Congregation decreed that the Society's teachers adhere to Aristotle not only in metaphysics and logic but in physics as well. Although in any vibrant organization there is always a certain discrepancy between practice and normative documents, in the Society the discrepancy had in this instance become distressingly acute. It was in this context, nonetheless, that the Jesuits produced Boscovich (1711–1787), who, among his other accomplishments, successfully labored for the abolition in 1757 of the Congregation of the Index's decree against the Copernican system.

As Aristotle lost credibility, other philosophers emerged and reconfigured the discipline. Descartes, the Jesuits' former pupil, was the first. The philosophical establishment rejected him to the point that the Paris Parlement threatened to ban his works. In 1663 his writings were placed on the papal Index "until corrected." They were nonetheless extremely influential and enjoyed great favor in learned circles well into the eighteenth century and beyond. Descartes failed, however, to win the support he hoped for from the Jesuits. The same was true for Spinoza, Leibniz, and others who succeeded him, even though individual Jesuits had cordial and reciprocally profitable relations with some of them.

The Age of the Enlightenment had dawned. By the end of the Thirty Years War in 1648, France had emerged as the unquestioned cultural capital of Europe. Although the Enlightenment had important proponents in Scotland, Germany, and elsewhere, even in North America, its epicenter was France. And it was in France that the positions normally associated with the Enlightenment, such as deism, freedom of religion, and the supreme authority of Reason, took forms that were viciously anti-Catholic. Voltaire's wish for the church was shared by many of his peers, *Ecrasons l'infâme!*

A clash between the Jesuits and the *philosophes*, as the spokesmen for Enlightenment ideals were known, was inevitable, especially since the latter recognized in the former their most able opponents. But the inevitability was not immediately evident. Beginning in 1701, the Jesuits published the *Journal de Trévoux*, a monthly that commented on the intellectual and cultural currents of the day. When the first volume of the *Encyclopédie* appeared in 1751, the *Journal* of course reviewed this first child of the publication considered the single most influential articulation of the ideals of the French Enlightenment.

The *Journal* gave the volume a positive review and greeted it as the beginning of a noble and mighty enterprise. As subsequent volumes appeared and their anti-Christian bias became more evident and pervasive, the *Journal* became of course ever more critical. Within a short while, therefore, the possibility of harmony between the Jesuits and the *philosophes*, whose influence by mid-century dominated intellectual culture in France, evanesced.

CONTROVERSY

During their second century, the Jesuits became the focal point of three major controversies of international scope, in each of which their opponents eventually triumphed. The first was the controversy over the degree of accommodation to Chinese culture that the Jesuits employed in their mission in Beijing, the famous "Chinese Rites" controversy. Even some Jesuits objected to the radical adaptation Ricci pioneered. But it was the Franciscans and Dominicans who first brought the issue into the international arena. They focused specifically on the Jesuits' willingness to allow converts to continue to practice traditional Chinese ceremonies honoring Confucius and their ancestors.

The controversy originated in the early 1640s when the first Spanish Dominicans and Franciscans entered China and were perplexed to witness Chinese converts to Christianity engaging in such rites. They questioned the Jesuit interpretation of the rites as civic, not religious. The friars then undertook their own investigation and came to conclusions at odds with the Jesuits'.

This divergence in interpretation assumed public and ominous importance in 1643. That year Juan Morales, a Dominican who opposed the Jesuit practice, submitted "Seventeen Questions" to the papacy. He described the rites in a way that could only evoke condemnation, which the Holy See in fact issued in 1645. In response to the condemnation, the Jesuits in China sent their own representative to Rome, Martino Martini, and in 1656, Pope Alexander VII through the Holy Office decided that the ceremonies as described by Martini were "a purely civil and political cult" and therefore admissible. But this second decree meant each side now had a papal document supporting its position, which left the situation ambiguous.

Twenty years later, in 1676, the controversy revived and entered an even more public phase when another Dominican, Domingo Fernández Navarrete, who had known the Jesuits in

China, published in Madrid his *Tratados . . . de la monarchia de China*, which was severely critical of the Jesuits' approach. The book, soon translated into several languages, became a major resource not only for those who had misgivings about the Jesuits' approach in China but for everybody with a grievance of any sort against the Society.

In the meantime the arrival in China of French clerics who were not Jesuits further tipped the balance against them. When in 1684 Charles Maigrot, Doctor of the Sorbonne and Vican Apostolic of Fujian, appeared on the scene, he immediately took a stand against the Jesuits. He provoked enormous ill will and resistance from the Chinese converts and of course from the Jesuits. The controversy moved into its final phase in 1697 when the Holy See agreed to consider the objections Maigrot raised against the Jesuits. The inquiry went on for seven years. The Jesuits reinforced their position by transmitting to Rome a declaration of Emperor Kangxi that the ceremonies were civic, not religious. They believed, wrongly, that the declaration was irrefutable proof of the correctness of their interpretation.

On November 20, 1704, Pope Clement XI issued a decree forbidding Catholics to participate in the rites. The decree did not directly repudiate the Jesuits' position that the rites were essentially civic, but it affirmed that in practice superstitions had become so entwined in them that they could not be allowed. Eleven years later the same pope issued a more resounding condemnation of the Jesuit position, which was in 1742 further confirmed by Pope Benedict XIV. No further appeal was possible.

The decree of 1704, promulgated in China by the papal legate there, Charles-Thomas Maillard de Tournon, was quite specific and forbade a long list of practices by then habitual in the Chinese church, such as the use of certain terms found in ancient Chinese classics to denote God, the use of the characters *jing tian* (respect heaven) bestowed by Kangxi to decorate churches, and of course, under pain of excommunication, participation in the "sacrificial" rites honoring Confucius and ancestors.

When Kangxi heard of the decision, he was furious, and in a reversal of his previously tolerant stance, he banned Christians from preaching in China. He continued, however, his cordial relations with the Jesuits, as shown by his engaging them for the great cartographical project. The Jesuits continued to hope against hope for a reversal of the decision, or a reversal of Kangxi's ban, but they did so in vain.

Despite Kangxi's continued friendship with the Jesuits, his ban was the great turning point. It marked the beginning of the end not only for the Jesuits in China but for all missionaries. It was the beginning of the end of Christianity there. Only in 1746, however, were anti-Christian laws carried out rigorously and the first missionaries executed, beginning with five Spanish Dominicans in 1747 and two Jesuits the next year. The Jesuits in Beijing managed to survive in ever diminishing numbers and less friendly circumstances. The last one did not die until 1805.

The paradox of the Rites Controversy is that it took place just as Sinophilia and its attendant Chinoiserie reached a peak in Europe. The phenomenon was due in large part to the letters from China the Jesuits wrote that were edited and published by their confreres in Europe and avidly read by a wide public. But papal condemnation of the rites gave the Jesuits' enemies the heaven-sent occasion they had been waiting for. They unleashed an avalanche of vilification of the Jesuits as betrayers of the Christian faith and teachers of the gospel of Confucius rather than the Gospel of

Christ, who in China amassed for themselves large fortunes. The Jansenists and the Paris Foreign Mission Society led the campaign. Michel Villermaules, an ardent Jansenist, published between 1733 and 1742 a seven-volume work that was nothing more than a collection of libels against the Jesuits, but his work was only one of many dozens of similar publications. The conclusion was inevitable: the only way to rid the church of the Jesuit scourge was to suppress the order altogether.

The damage done to the Society by the "Chinese Rites" controversy was compounded by the "Malabar Rites" controversy that occurred at roughly the same time in South India. De Tournon had spent eight months in Pondicherry (Puducherry) on his way to China. Just before he left he issued a decree forbidding certain accommodations the Jesuits made, especially in administering baptism and visiting sick pariahs in the homes. The Jesuits pleaded their cause with him and with the Holy See in a case that dragged on until 1744 when Pope Benedict XIV allowed some of the Jesuit practices and forbade others. By this time, however, the Jesuits' enemies in Europe had seized the Malabar Rites as another instance of Jesuit disobedience and selling out to paganism.

The second major controversy was the direct confrontation of the Jesuits with the Jansenists. Its point of origin was Louvain, where in 1640 Cornelis Jansen's *Augustinus* was published posthumously. Jansen, who hoped to save the Catholic Church from the moral laxity of the Jesuits and make it into a model of probity that would lead to the conversion of Dutch Calvinists, turned to Saint Augustine, whose entire corpus he purportedly read ten times in preparation for the book. He had come to believe from the earlier *De auxiliis* controversy in Spain that the Jesuits by their emphasis on free will denied the efficacy of grace in the struggle against sin and that they subscribed to the Pelagianism that Augustine had so strenuously opposed and early councils of the church so clearly condemned.

The Belgian Jesuits tried to halt the publication of the *Augustinus* and, when that failed, to have it condemned in Rome. They found its doctrine scarcely distinguishable from Calvinism, and, in fact, the Jansenists began to embody a religious culture and moral rigor that resembled Puritanism. The friends and partisans of Jansen, especially those in France, led by Antoine Arnauld (1612–1694), reacted to the Jesuits with the ferocity to be expected under the circumstances and set in motion the idea that the Jesuits were responsible for every setback the Jansenists received from either secular or religious authorities.

The atmosphere turned acrid as anti-Jansenist and anti-Jesuit factions rapidly formed and as the controversy grew in France to engage the Paris Parlement and even the crown. Although the epicenter for the controversy had fast become Paris, for well over a hundred years Jansenism took deep hold in aristocratic lay and clerical circles throughout Europe, including members of the papal court itself.

The Jansenists soon came to define themselves almost in opposition to the Jesuits. Their grievances against them fell under six main headings. The first was the Jesuits' more optimistic assessment of human nature and free will, in contrast to the Jansenists' doctrine of the utter corruption of human nature by Original Sin and the resulting powerlessness of the will to do good. The second, closely related, was the Jesuits' advocacy of frequent reception of the Eucharist, which according to the Jansenists was incompatible with human unworthiness.

The third was the Jesuits' reconciliation with almost every aspect of classical culture, a symptom of the Jesuits' worldliness that was most blatantly manifest in their promotion in their schools of theater and dance. It was also manifest in the Jesuits' employment of "pagan magnificence" in their various enterprises and especially in what for the Jansenists was the overwrought character of the Jesuits' baroque churches.

The reconciliation with the pagan cultures of ancient Greece and Rome was related to the analogous reconciliation the Jesuits attempted with the cultures of Japan and China, an abuse passionately and unremittingly denounced by the Jansenists even long after the promulgation of the papal decrees against the rites. This was the fourth grievance. The fifth was the Jesuits' pride and arrogance so evident in everything they did, beginning with the audacity of the very name of the Society.

The final grievance was the Jesuits' adoption of probabilism as their preferred form of moral reasoning. Jesuits (and others) who subscribed to probabilism taught that, in a conflict of opinion among respected theologians over the morality or immorality of a given act, the confessor was obliged to give the penitent the benefit of the less rigorous opinion, even if that opinion was regarded as less probable. The Jansenists saw the Jesuits' advocacy of probabilism as proof positive of their moral laxity. Probabilism was an abomination that condoned sin and destroyed public morality. It was a devious device that enabled the Jesuits to win favor, especially with the mighty, by finding ways to let penitents wiggle out of responsibility for wrongdoing.

In 1643, just three years after the publication of the *Augustinus*, Arnauld, brilliant member of a well-known and distinguished French family, published two anti-Jesuit works, *Théologie morale des jésuites* and *De la fréquente communion*. These were just the beginning of the anti-Jesuit works inspired by the Jansenists that henceforth poured from the presses especially in France and that became ever more vitriolic. Not vitriol, however, but understated wit and elegant style made Pascal's *Lettres Provinciales* all the more effective in their parody of the Jesuits. The *Lettres*, published between 1656 and 1657, remains one of the most accomplished satires in the history of literature.

For Pascal, as for other Jansenists, the Jesuits were compromisers who betrayed the purity of the Gospel message and preached an easy road to salvation. The most obvious manifestation of the Jesuits' moral laxity was their advocacy of probabilism. Jesuit theologians published a large number of books in which they argued about the possible moral assessments of particular cases in which there seemed to be a conflict of moral principles. These theologians, not all of whom argued their positions well, were Pascal's specific target.

In the fictitious *Lettres*, their supposed author, curious about the Jesuits, consults one of them, who turns out to be well-meaning and eager to answer questions but hopelessly naive. The Jesuit reassures his questioner that the members of his order are flexible enough to be severe with penitents who like that sort of thing but able to give wide latitude to others. As the author probes, it becomes clear that the Jesuit does not see the implications of the positions he has been schooled to defend or realize how at odds they are with the true standards of the Gospel championed by the Jansenists.

The *Lettres* along with the *Monita Secreta* turned out to be in the long run the most successful of all anti-Jesuit writings. The

light and witty style of the *Lettres*, besides embodying and promoting a shift in what constituted "good taste," was destined to win
for the Jansenists a following in readers who were otherwise
repelled by their severe and rigid moral standards.

Pascal was far from being the only Jansenist to use satire
against the Jesuits. Isaac-Louis Lemaistre de Sacy (1619–1684),
best known for his French translation of the Bible, was a nephew
of Arnauld and a close friend of Pascal's. In 1654 he published
anonymously *Les enluminures du fameus almanach des PP. Iesuistes*
[*sic*]. In it he in verse makes devastating fun, for instance, of the
Jesuits' spiritual teaching as sweet and civilized. The style of piety
the Jesuits promote is gallant, pretty, polite, and nicely coiffured.
It makes people devout *à la mode*:

> Elle est douce & civilisée
> Et mesle aux bonnes actions
> Les belles conversations,
> Elle est galante, elle est jolie,
> Elle est frizée, elle est polie
> Elle marche avec cet agrément
> Plus à l'aise & plus seurement
> Elle rend devot à la mode.

But the battle went beyond words. In the wake of the furor
in France over *Unigenitus*, the last major papal bull condemning
Jansenism, a Jesuit preached an anti-Jansenist sermon. In retaliation
Louis-Antoine de Noailles, archbishop of Paris and the leading
figure in France trying to circumvent the bull, published in 1716
an edict prohibiting the Jesuits in Paris from preaching, hearing
confessions, and practicing any other ministry. This extraordinarily
severe edict remained in force for thirteen years, until Noailles's
death in 1729.

Jansenism, though condemned by the Holy See, never lost its appeal in certain quarters and remained a small but extraordinarily powerful force in continental Catholicism until just after the French Revolution. For the Jansenists the destruction of the Jesuits grew to an obsession. By the last quarter of the eighteenth century, they were able to enter into informal alliances with the Jesuits' other enemies to accomplish their goal.

The third great controversy concerned the reductions in Paraguay. By 1767 there were thirty of them with a population of some 110,000 natives, especially the Guaraní, in the territory of present-day Paraguay, Argentina, Bolivia, Uruguay, and Brazil. They were, as mentioned, overseen by a small handful of Jesuits. This "Republic," as they came to be known, aroused great curiosity in Europe, where it was much admired and sometimes idealized even by *philosophes*.

Protection of the natives from the raids upon them by Spanish and Portuguese slave traders was a primary motivation for the establishment of the reductions. But these unarmed settlements could not resist the armed attacks of the marauders, who prowled the jungles looking for natives to enslave. In 1628 the kidnappers devastated the area of Guayrá, left intact only two of the eleven reductions, and reduced the original population from one hundred thousand to twelve thousand.

In 1637 the Jesuit Antonio Ruiz de Montoya went to Madrid, where he was successful in obtaining royal permission to arm the natives, who then were able to defend themselves. The raids came virtually to an end. However, this expedient evoked fear in government circles of a potentially rebellious army, and in 1661 Philip V ordered firearms withdrawn from the reductions. The Jesuits obeyed, but when the raids began again with great devastation, the crown had to renew the permission.

From that point forward all seemed well, but since the reductions operated virtually independently of the royal governors and even the hierarchy, those authorities resented them, envied their prosperity, and therefore wanted to wrest control from the Jesuits. As rumors spread that in the reductions the Jesuits operated secret gold mines and gunpowder plants, the pressure to intervene increased accordingly. Spanish settlers, moreover, resented the economic competition from the sale of products from the reductions, which operated much more efficiently than their competitors, and complained that the Amerindians were undertaxed.

The crisis came in 1750. That year Spain and Portugal signed the Treaty of Madrid for an exchange of territory in America. This treaty, not particularly momentous in itself, initiated the process that led to the complete destruction of the Jesuit achievement in Latin America and was the first step leading to the suppression of the Society itself. Located in the territory Spain ceded to Portugal were seven reductions with about thirty thousand natives. According to the treaty, the natives had to abandon their homes and move to Spanish territory.

The Jesuits protested the injustice of the terms, the violation of the Indians' rights, and the virtual impossibility of such a massive movement of humanity through jungles and over rough terrain without serious loss of life. Their appeals failed. The Jesuits were now caught between obedience to the crown, whose position their superior general supported, and their commitment to the welfare of the Indians. When they finally attempted to get the migration moving, the Indians reacted with bitterness. When in 1754 Spanish and Portuguese troops tried to seize the reductions, the Indians replied in kind and set off the so-called War of the Seven Reductions. Not until 1756 were the Indians defeated and the seven reductions seized, which ultimately led to their dissolution.

CALAMITY

In Lisbon the Marquis de Pombal, prime minister to King Joseph I, seized upon the war as an occasion to prove the Jesuits' disloyalty to the crown, which according to him was only one of their many crimes. He did not let up. In 1758 he demanded that Pope Benedict XIV end the Jesuits' disobedience in the church, their thirst for power, their lust for gold, and their insatiable hunger for land. A brief and cursory papal investigation of the Jesuits in Portugal ensued and, without examination of a single account book, concluded the Jesuits were guilty of financial malfeasance.

Then, on the night of September 3 that same year, an attempt was made on the king's life. Pombal saw his chance. He accused the Jesuits of complicity in a plot against the king and won Joseph I over to his side. In January the next year, 1759, the king ordered the confiscation of all Jesuit property, and on September 3, first anniversary of the failed regicide, he decreed the expulsion of the Jesuits, rebels and traitors, from his realms, which of course included the Portuguese territories overseas. Soon rallying to the government's anti-Jesuit policy were a number of high prelates, creatures of the crown, who now fixed their eyes on Jesuit buildings and other resources.

The Jesuits in Portugal were herded onto ships that carried some 1,100 of them to Italy where, uninvited, they hoped to find refuge. Another 180 from the missions were not so lucky. Transported to Portugal, they were stuffed into underground dungeons where they were left to rot away. The most publicized act to show to the world the Jesuits' disloyalty took place in Rossio Square in Lisbon on September 20, 1761, when Gabriele Malagrida, an aged and by then mentally confused Jesuit accused of plotting against the king's life, was brutally strangled and burned at the stake.

Pombal's action against the Jesuits must be explained on several levels. It fed his pride and ambition by showing he was able to bring down such an established institution. It enriched the crown through the seizure of the Jesuits' properties and institutions. For Pombal, a creature of the Enlightenment, the elimination of the Jesuits fit a larger plan to eradicate from the land the superstition that was Catholicism and to humiliate the papacy by showing it was powerless to protect the Jesuits. His success had an impact far beyond Portugal and the Portuguese dominions. It demonstrated to Europe both the vulnerability of the supposedly powerful Society of Jesus and the papacy's impotence to protect it.

The first step in the destruction of the Jesuit pest had been taken. The next step was taken by France, the key nation on the continent, where the Gallican sentiments of both clergy and laity sat ill with a religious order whose headquarters were in Rome. Pervasive though Gallican sentiments were, they were only one of the forces that, though often at odds with one another, made common cause against the Jesuits. The *philosophes*, for instance, despised the Jansenists but found themselves in the same camp with them when it came to the Jesuits.

The magistrates of the Paris Parlement, moreover, looked for occasions to put restraints on the absolute authority claimed by the Bourbon monarchs. Like his predecessors beginning with Henry IV, the reigning Louis XV favored and protected the Jesuits. To force him to act against them would be a triumph for the magistrates, many of whom were Jansenists. The hour was ripe. The king's prestige and authority had been severely damaged by defeats during the Seven Years War, just when he badly needed his Parlements to approve new taxes.

Two events provided the anti-Jesuit forces with the catalyst they needed to go into action. In January 1757, Louis XV was stabbed in the courtyard of Versailles by a man who had been a pupil of the Jesuits. Although the man claimed he was inspired to his deed from what he had heard from a Jansenist magistrate, public opinion was manipulated to incriminate the Jesuits. After all, the propaganda ran, the Jesuits had been proved responsible for the attempt on Joseph I of Portugal. When news of Malagrida's execution in Lisbon in 1761 reached Paris, it was greeted as vindication of the accusations against the Jesuits.

The second was a notorious case that had dragged on in the law courts for six years until finally decided against the Jesuits by the Paris Parlement in 1761. The Jesuit Antoine Lavalette (or Valette), superior of the French mission in Martinique, began taking dangerous chances in order to relieve the heavy debt of the mission. His ability to meet payments to his debtors depended on selling the produce of the mission in Europe. Unfortunately, in 1756 English corsairs swooped down on the thirteen ships he had hired for a shipment, so that only one of his cargoes reached Cádiz. Creditors demanded payment and sued the Society of Jesus in France. Not only did the Jesuits lose the case, but "the Lavalette affair" was paraded as proof positive of the Jesuits' loose morals and lust for gold.

Three months after the decision against Lavalette, the Paris Parlement took action. It ordered that the Jesuits' schools be closed and that the works of twenty-three Jesuit authors, including Bellarmino and Suárez, be burned. The king intervened, and in the ensuing months the royal council devised several plans to save the Society, which were repugnant to both the Jesuits and the Parlement and, hence, unavailing.

On August 6, 1762, the Paris Parlement declared that the Society of Jesus, destroyer of religion and morality, was barred from France. In separate decrees it ordered Jesuits to abandon all relations with the Society and made them ineligible for any academic or civic positions unless they publicly repudiated it. Just as severe and laden with almost irreversible consequences, another decree declared all Jesuit buildings, institutions, and properties confiscated.

In Paris steps were immediately taken to implement the decrees, but at least for a while in other parts of France, some parlements resisted the pressure from Paris. But the die was cast. Finally, in November 1764, Louis XV, his hand forced, took the final step and issued the royal decree of suppression. In it he mitigated the conditions the Parlement had laid down for the Jesuits, but even the mitigation could not save some three thousand Jesuits from destitution. Ejected from their communities and all their assets seized, they had to find food and shelter wherever they could, as best they could.

Spain soon followed suit. The monarchy had a long tradition of asserting Spanish rights against the encroachments of Rome. King Charles III, surrounded by advisers who believed the Jesuits were subversive of those rights, became thoroughly convinced that the Society was the monster its enemies described. Encouraged by the example of Portugal and France, he decided to eject from his domains the Jesuits, notorious fomenters of rebellion. On January 29, 1767, the Extraordinary Council ordered the banishment of the Society of Jesus from all Spanish territory and the seizure of all its properties.

The king declared any public protest in favor of the Jesuits an act of high treason, punishable by death. The Jesuits in Spain and overseas were forced onto ships and sent onto the high seas, destination unspecified. Only at that point did Spanish officials open negotiations about where they might deposit their unwanted cargo. The refugees themselves, which included some 1,800 from the overseas missions, bounced from port to port, where one after another refused them admittance.

The Kingdom of the Two Sicilies (Naples) and the Duchy of Parma were the next to banish the Jesuits, but the great prize, a general suppression by the papacy, eluded the Jesuits' enemies. Such a suppression would not only rid the whole church of the Jesuits but show to all the world the weakness of the papacy. Pope Clement XIII (reigned 1758–1769) took action many times to try to forestall the suppression in France alone, and he publicly testified to the innocence of the Jesuits and their extraordinary importance for the well-being of the church.

When on February 15, 1769, the conclave to elect his successor opened, the Jesuit question immediately dominated it, which was one of the lengthiest and most contentious conclaves in recent history. Only after three months and a virtually unprecedented 185 voting sessions was Clement XIV elected. When word arrived at the court of Charles III in Spain, a solemn Te Deum was sung in gratitude. Although the new pope seems not openly to have promised to suppress the Jesuits, he could hardly have been elected without somehow communicating a readiness to do so. Nonetheless, he held off for four years. The pressure upon him, which included the implicit threat of schism if he failed to act, was intense. Finally, on July 21, 1773, he signed the brief *Dominus ac Redemptor* abolishing the Society of Jesus—"for the peace and tranquility of the church."

The document, forty-five paragraphs long, consists in an indictment of the Jesuits and a justification of the pope's action. Then come the fateful words, "We suppress and abolish the said Society; we deprive it of all activity whatever, and we likewise deprive it of its houses, schools, colleges, hospitals, lands . . . in whatever kingdom or province they may be situated." The document strictly forbade Jesuits to comment on the decree, criticize it, or appeal it.

In many places *Dominus ac Redemptor* became the warrant for an orgy of systematic and officially sanctioned looting. In Belgium the devastation was particularly severe. From the Jesuit houses, officials seized about thirty valuable paintings by Rubens, Van Dyck, Brueghel, and others and sent them to the imperial galleries in Vienna, where they remain to this day. They gutted the libraries. Of some five hundred thousand volumes, they classified 75 percent as theological rubbish and sold them for wastepaper. In Naples the avid search for Jesuit gold uncovered, instead, a debt of 200,000 ducats.

A month after the formal publication of *Dominus ac Redemptor*, papal officials and police entered Jesuit headquarters in Rome; arrested the superior general, Lorenzo Ricci, and his assistants ("the Jesuit Sanhedrin," as their enemies called them); and, after sequestering them briefly in the Venerable English College, imprisoned them in Castel Sant'Angelo. The jailers there refused Ricci permission to write, boarded up his windows, cut his food rations in half, and in winter denied him heat. No specific charges were ever able to be proved against him, and the 50 million scudi he was accused of hoarding turned out never to have existed. He died two years later, still a prisoner in Castel Sant'Angelo and still protesting the innocence of the Society.

4

THE MODERN AND
POSTMODERN ERA

The suppression of the Society of Jesus was a tragedy for the Jesuits but also a tragedy for the church at large. Within the space of less than fifteen years—from the Portuguese suppression in 1759 until the papal in 1773—the single greatest intellectual asset the church possessed was wiped out, as the Jesuits' libraries were dispersed and their network of more than seven hundred schools closed or passed into secular hands. The Jesuits were as a body the most broadly learned clergy in the church, no matter what may have been the limitations of their intellectual culture.

The Society of Jesus as a corporate force was no more. Compounding the calamity was the fact that the suppression occurred just as European culture was rapidly moving into unprecedentedly new forms, many of which were hostile to Christianity and particularly hostile to Catholicism. This was a moment when the church needed to husband and nurture its best resources, not a moment to see them dispersed and lost. As events turned out, the suppression of the Jesuits presaged the devastations soon visited upon other orders as a result of the social and political upheavals that in 1773 were just beyond the horizon.

If individual Jesuits were lucky enough to escape exile and prison, they were still scattered, dispossessed of their houses, and forced to fend for themselves. Although some fared reasonably well by entering the diocesan clergy or otherwise finding means to support themselves, many never recovered from the disorientation, the mental anguish, and the sense of loss the situation caused them.

THE ROAD TO RESTORATION

The suppressions and expulsions before 1773 in Portugal, France, Spain, and elsewhere were implemented consistently and often brutally by the governments that decreed them, but the same was not always true for the papal suppression. Unlike them, this one demanded formal promulgation by the bishop of every diocese in which a Jesuit community existed. More important, this suppression did not originate with the civil authorities, to whom, however, the papacy now entrusted the responsibility for carrying it out. These authorities often felt less committed to the undertaking and perhaps even unhappy with it. They sometimes treated the former Jesuits more gently. Since, however, by the terms of *Dominus ac Redemptor* these disgraced clerics could not accept novices, they were doomed to eventual extinction.

In the English colonies in North America, soon to be the United States, the civil authorities, who were all either Protestants or Deists, had not the slightest intention of implementing a papal brief. They therefore took no measures against the twenty or so Jesuits living there, who were still the only Catholic priests in that vast area. But in late 1773 the Jesuits themselves, upon receiving the shocking news of the suppression, signed and sent to Rome a document declaring their "obedience and submission" to the provisions of the decree.

Although the American Jesuits no longer called themselves Jesuits, they eventually organized themselves into a civilly recognized institution that enabled them to hold onto their assets and to continue their ministries to the thirty thousand Catholics there precisely as they had always done. As they looked forward to the day the Society might be restored, they, under the leadership of Bishop John Carroll, one of their number, took those ministries a step further by founding in 1789 a school on the banks of the Potomac River, Georgetown Academy. It was the first Catholic school in the United States, and it professedly opened its doors to persons of all religious faiths.

Two rulers refused outright to allow the papal brief to be implemented. By his conquests in Poland and Silesia, Frederick the Great of Prussia had absorbed into his realm thirteen Jesuit colleges and seven residences. Although he was thoroughly imbued with the principles of the Enlightenment, he had come to admire the Jesuits and did not want to lose them as teachers. The Holy See insisted with him that the Society be dissolved, but in 1776 as a compromise the new pope, Pius VI, allowed the ex-Jesuits to function corporately under the bishops. This "Institute" was, however, finally dissolved by the Prussian government in 1800.

Of lasting and pivotal significance, however, was the refusal of Catherine the Great of Russia to implement Clement XIV's decree. As a result of the First Partition of Poland, 1772, Catherine came into possession of territory in what is today Belarus and with it into possession of four colleges and two residences staffed by two hundred Jesuits. Like Frederick she appreciated the contribution the Jesuits made to cultural life, and, imperious person that she was, she saw no reason to implement in her empire a decree from a foreign government.

Catherine's refusal to carry out the suppression threw her Jesuit subjects into a moral dilemma: how were they to deal with *Dominus ac Redemptor*? Were they not obliged somehow to suppress themselves? Feeling ever more oppressed by the ambiguity of the situation, they through their superior Stanisław Czerniewicz appealed in 1776 for guidance to Pius VI. The pope worried about reaction from the western monarchies that had demanded the suppression. Although he reassured them that *Dominus ac Redemptor* was still fully in force, he at the same time seemed willing to turn a blind eye to what was happening in Catherine's realms. He replied to Czerniewicz enigmatically, "May the result of your prayers, as I foresee and you desire, be a happy one."

Czerniewicz now felt reasonably confident that the pope's reply allowed him in good conscience to move ahead. He shortly thereafter informed the empress that because the Jesuits' numbers had fallen by 25 percent since 1773, they could not continue their work unless they were allowed to receive novices to replenish their ranks. Through Catherine's clever diplomacy, the Holy See was maneuvered into granting permission for the founding of a novitiate. The Jesuits' enemies in Portugal, France, and especially Spain fell into a rage and protested to the empress, but she refused to back down. On February 2, 1780, just seven years after *Dominus ac Redemptor*, the novitiate opened at Połotsk with eight novices.

Within another three years, Pius VI gave to Catherine's envoy in Rome his verbal approval of what was taking place in Russia. With that, the Jesuits mounted a full program of training and education for new members that replicated the program in force in the Society prior to 1773. They now assumed that they constituted the Society of Jesus in miniature and elected Czernie-wicz as, in effect, the superior general of the order. When Catherine died in 1796, her successor Paul I continued to support the Jesuits. Suppressed worldwide, the Society by a strange twist of fate survived intact in Russia—or, perhaps better put, in Poland.

When the French Revolution broke out, the Society's ene-mies—the kings and their ministers in France, Spain, and Portu-gal—had a more pressing and immediate problem than the survival of the Jesuits: their own survival was now in mortal danger. At least regarding the Jesuits, this situation left the papacy freer to act than before. On March 17, 1801, Pope Pius VII, the newly elected successor to Pius VI, officially confirmed in his brief *Catholicae fidei* the existence of the Society in Russia and thus dispelled any doubts about the legitimacy of what had taken place.

With *Catholicae fidei* Pius VII took the crucial step toward what he hoped to accomplish, the full restoration of the Society. Groups of former Jesuits as well as younger men with no previous association with the Society now had an institution with which they could affiliate. Thus did the Society become officially rees-tablished, for instance, in England in 1803, in the Kingdom of the Two Sicilies in 1804, and with the few ex-Jesuits still surviving in the United States in 1805.

Even some former enemies of the Society who had demanded its suppression regretted what had happened and petitioned the pope to bring back the Jesuits. In the Catholic world, now shaken to its depths by the French Revolution and its Europe-wide aftermath, the tide had turned in the Jesuits' favor. Finally, on August 7, 1814, Pius VII, after celebrating mass in Rome at the altar of Saint Ignatius in the church of the Gesù, decreed through the bull *Sollicitudo omnium ecclesiarum* the universal restoration of the Society of Jesus.

THE RESTORED SOCIETY OF JESUS

The Society had been reborn, but reborn into a world vastly different from the world at the time of the suppressions. The Industrial Revolution was under way and gaining force, with the radical changes it would bring about in almost every aspect of human life. But more dramatic and more immediate in awareness was the French Revolution. It had toppled monarchs from their thrones and proclaimed an era of liberty, equality, and fraternity. Even though with less devastating impact than in France, the Revolution affected every country in western Europe, as well as in French, Portuguese, and Spanish America. It shook the foundations of all their institutions.

To save itself from bankruptcy, the new government in France confiscated the entire property of the French church and engaged in a massive sell-off not only of sacred vessels, paintings, and furnishings but even of real estate. With the Reign of Terror, recalcitrant bishops and priests were guillotined or drowned as punishment for their treason. Churches were sacked, some left in ruins. In 1798 the French occupied Rome and took Pius VI prisoner to France, where he died the next year. In 1809 Napoleon did the same to Pius VII and held him at Savona and then Fontainebleau until 1814.

In that very year of 1814, the counterrevolutionary forces brought Napoleon to his knees and thus stopped the seemingly unstoppable French juggernaut. Those forces met in the Congress of Vienna, 1814–1815, where they restored to their thrones all monarchs, including the papal monarch, and in other ways tried to turn the clock back to the institutions and values of the *ancien régime*. But the clock and large numbers of people resisted, which meant that nineteenth-century Europe experienced a seesaw between forms of republican and monarchical government, which partisans in each camp defended with intransigent ideologies.

The leadership of the Catholic Church, and especially papal leadership, soon came down unequivocally on the side of the *ancien régime*, which meant opposition to virtually everything that now began to proclaim itself modern. Liberty, equality, and fraternity became anathema to devout Catholics, who saw in the slogan nothing but a recipe for chaos and carnage. More moderate voices tried to make themselves heard, but generally to little avail.

This was the context in which the restoration of the Society of Jesus occurred. The young men who now entered it were perforce creatures of that context. Although there were exceptions, the Jesuits of the nineteenth and early twentieth centuries were inimical to the values of "the modern world" or at least highly skeptical of them.

The Jesuits' main efforts, however, were directed to putting their own house in order and especially to once again taking up their ministries. They did their best, often under the most adverse circumstances, to reconstruct the traditions operative before the suppressions severed them many decades earlier. To guide them, however, they had available only a small number of texts, virtually all of them normative: the *Spiritual Exercises*, the *Constitutions*, the *Ratio Studiorum*, and a selection of the letters of Saint Ignatius. They also had specific ordinances of more recent fathers general and detailed rules regulating daily life, and such documents as these loomed large in how Jesuits began to think of their vocation. "Observing the rules" sometimes seemed to be the essence of the Jesuit vocation.

The vast correspondence of the early Jesuits had either been looted and scattered at the time of the suppressions or, at best, lay unexamined in the archives the Society in some places now had restored to it. Missing in the Society's attempt to re-create itself were the traditions as they were actually lived. The result was an often wooden, moralistic, and legalistic interpretation of the normative texts. But the discrepancy between such interpretations and the way life had to be lived made itself felt ever more keenly.

In 1814 there were about six hundred Jesuits, virtually all of them in Europe. Not until six years later was the Twentieth General Congregation able to meet to elect a new superior general. After a contentious beginning, the delegates chose the seventy-two-year-old Italian Luigi Fortis. By then the number of Jesuits had already doubled, but it was still a pitifully small number compared with the 22,500 in the middle of the previous century. For nine years Fortis worked quietly but effectively at putting in place the necessary institutions within the Society for it to be able to function.

By the time Fortis died, the number of Jesuits had again doubled. By midcentury it reached five thousand and by 1900 about fifteen thousand. In 1900 the Dominicans had been reduced to just over four thousand, and the combined branches of the Franciscans to only a few thousand more than the Jesuits. The Carmelites and Augustinians were operating at less than 20 percent of their numbers before the Revolution. In this scenario, therefore, the Jesuits were doing very well.

They were fortunate in that Fortis's two successors had long tenures, which provided stability to an organization still finding its way. Jan Roothan, general from 1829 to 1853, exercised an especially important influence during his tenure of twenty-four years because he called Jesuits' attention to the centrality of the *Spiritual Exercises* in their spirituality and in an important letter in 1833 impressed upon them the need to revive the Society's missionary tradition. He brought to completion, as well, a revision and updating of the *Ratio Studiorum*, but, as time would tell, even the revision did not meet the new and rapidly evolving needs and expectations of prospective students. The Jesuits attempted, as was typical of them, to meet those needs and expectations and bit by bit put a distance between practice and norm.

They set about their ministries with energy and enthusiasm. In the Papal States and in a few other places, they received back some of their original real estate and buildings, but for the most part they had to begin from scratch. In no area of endeavor was this more difficult than the schools because of the investment of men, money, and ongoing commitment they required. Nonetheless, the Jesuits succeeded remarkably well, especially in times and places where they enjoyed the favor of the government. Their schools once again began to enjoy prestige, especially among the upper classes for whom the limitations of the *Ratio*, rather than being a problem, symbolized the restoration of the standards of an earlier and happier time.

The schools, as well as the other ministries, of course suffered severely from the political upheavals in Catholic countries that marked the nineteenth and early twentieth centuries. The Jesuits, now identified by friend and foe as among the strongest supporters of the older order, that is, of monarchy or its equivalent, were expelled from country after country only to return with a change of regime. France, for instance, banished them three times—in 1828, 1880, and 1901. At the time of the banishment in 1901, the Jesuits had to leave behind twenty-four colleges as well as churches and other institutions. As before, they had to seek refuge abroad.

France was hardly unique. Spain expelled the Jesuits in 1835 and 1868, and Germany in 1872. Besides other European countries, Colombia banished them in 1850, Guatemala in 1871, Nicaragua in 1881, and Brazil in 1889. Between 1821 and 1914, the Jesuits had to leave Mexico five times. In 1873 after the seizure of Rome by the forces of the new Kingdom of Italy, Pieter Jan Beckx, Roothan's successor as general, took refuge in Fiesole outside Florence. Not until twenty-two years later, 1895, when Luis Martín was general, would the Jesuit curia be able to return to Rome. In Italy and elsewhere, anti-Jesuit vitriol flourished. It was for the most part an update of the themes of the *Monita Secreta*.

As a certainly unintended consequence, the expulsions helped supply manpower for the Society's missions. Banished from their homelands, the exiled Jesuits had a new freedom to heed the call of the superiors general to venture into new lands. The nineteenth and early twentieth centuries saw waves of missionaries setting out from Europe for Asia, Africa, and America, some because they needed to seek a new home but others simply inspired by the example of earlier Jesuit missionaries, especially Francisco Xavier. Not only among Jesuits but among Catholics at large, Xavier became one of the era's most popular saints, much better known and revered than Saint Ignatius. The Jesuits were again giving substance to their claim that "the world is our house."

The Society returned to China in 1842 when two French Jesuits landed in Shanghai. As their numbers increased, the old problem of Chinese Rites returned because a ceremony honoring Confucius was required of everybody entering government service. After the revolution of 1911–1912, the new government declared the act was of purely civil significance. Twenty-five years later, the Holy See abrogated the old prohibition. By 1945 more than nine hundred Jesuits were in China, of whom 250 were Chinese. But Chinese suspicion and resentment of foreigners exploded time and again, culminating with the expulsion of all Christian missionaries by the Communist government in 1949.

To Japan the Jesuits returned late, only when asked by Pope Pius X to found a university there. In 1914 they opened Sophia University in Tokyo, which especially after World War II achieved a distinguished reputation. In India the Jesuits arrived in considerable numbers and on an international basis. The Belgians went to Bengal and Ceylon (Sri Lanka), the French to Malabar and Madurai, the Germans to Bombay (Mumbai), the Italians to Mangalore. The Americans and Canadians arrived much later in Darjeeling, Jamshedpur, and Patna. As before, the Jesuits established schools, seminaries, printing presses, and churches wherever they went. These institutions soon flourished and continue to do so today in a country that now boasts eighteen Jesuit provinces, the largest number in a single country in the whole history of the Society.

In the United States the Society experienced extraordinary success, even though it was a nation with a strong anti-Catholic prejudice. Immigrants from Catholic countries of Europe began arriving in great numbers, and with them came priests, including a significant number of Jesuits. By the middle of the century, Jesuits from Flemish Belgium had settled in the midwestern part of the country, from France in Louisiana and other parts of the south, from Italy in the west. Later in the century came more Italians for the southwest, Germans for the area of the Great Lakes, and Irish for the northeast. They established schools in virtually every major city where they were present and used them to help integrate into American society the sons of immigrants. By century's end, the Society in the United States numbered close to two thousand members.

European Jesuits also arrived in significant numbers in the various countries of Latin America, where they found a situation that resembled what they had left behind—the Catholic heritage now radically challenged by an anticlerical Liberalism, the generic name for republican and secular ideologies. The political situation tended, therefore, to be as unstable as in parts of Europe and often rabidly unfavorable to the Jesuits. Nonetheless, by 1900 there were about 1,500 Jesuits working there, many of them Europeans.

The Jesuits had been in Africa since the beginning, but for a variety of reasons their missions there never really stabilized. That was now no longer true. French Jesuits arrived in Madagascar in 1844, for instance, and the Belgians in the Congo (Zaire or Congo Kinshasa) in 1893. In that same year the British province took over the mission to present-day Zimbabwe from Jesuits from various provinces who had arrived there a few years earlier. As was true of other missionaries of the era, the Jesuits traveled under the flags of their respective nations and tended to see themselves as promoting the culture and values of the home country in what was both a religious and a "civilizing" mission. This aspect of their labors changed radically after World War II.

By the early decades of the twentieth century, therefore, the Jesuits once again seemed to be everywhere, even in what might seem like highly unlikely places. In 1914, for instance, there were 217 in Armenia and Syria, 22 in Egypt, 78 in Indonesia, 102 in Australia, and 42 in Albania. In these places and wherever they were, they tried to learn the languages and, in accordance with their tradition, to accommodate as best they could to local situations.

The Jesuits of this era did something that, except for the *Journal de Trévoux*, their predecessors never did. In most countries where they established themselves, they began publishing journals and periodicals aimed at both professional and general readerships. Some in the latter category were devotional. Others were important commentaries on contemporary politics, religion, and culture, such as *La Civiltà Cattolica*, 1850, in Italy; *Études*, 1856, in France; and *Stimmen aus Maria Laach*, 1871 (since 1914, *Stimmen der Zeit*), in Germany—all of which are still publishing today. From 1865 until 2001, the English Jesuits published *The Month*, a journal whose pages contained contributions from such distinguished authors as John Henry Newman, Evelyn Waugh, Graham Greene, Edith Sitwell, and Muriel Spark.

The Jesuits continued to cultivate the sciences. Some schools around the world again began to operate astronomical observatories, as had their predecessors, and they provided a welcome service to the discipline until the cost of keeping up with technological advances became prohibitive. Even today the Society still trains a few members to staff the Vatican's Observatory, where the equipment is up to present-day standards. The best-known Jesuit scientist in the modern era is of course Pierre Teilhard de Chardin (1881–1955), the French paleontologist.

THE EARLY TWENTIETH CENTURY

The introduction of historical methods into the study of virtually all disciplines is one of the most striking features of the intellectual culture of the nineteenth century. Jesuits at first resisted the application of these methods to sacred subjects. In the early twentieth century the general, Luis Martín, enthusiastically supported Pope Pius X's campaign against Modernism, a movement among Catholic intellectuals in which such an application was a pervasive characteristic.

But by the 1930s and 1940s, some Jesuits had become leaders in the enterprise. For a revival of the theology of the patristic era, for instance, the Belgian Jesuit Émile Mersch (1890–1940) and the French Jesuit Henri de Lubac (1896–1991) played important roles and challenged the theological paradigm in vogue that was based on medieval Scholasticism. In 1932 the Austrian Jesuit Josef Andreas Jungmann (1889–1975) published a book showing that the Catholic discipline of requiring private confession to a priest for the forgiveness of sins was unknown until the Middle Ages. Then in 1948 he published his groundbreaking and extremely influential *Missarum Solemnia*, a study of the history of the mass of the Roman rite showing the changes that had occurred over the centuries. For the Catholic Church and therefore for the Society of Jesus, studies like these had an incalculably great impact and required a reexamination of established traditions.

As Jesuits applied the new methods to the history of the Society itself, the methods had a transforming impact on the development of Jesuit self-understanding. They made the tradition available in an incomparably broader base of documents, which led to a broader understanding of it. A group of Spanish Jesuits under the leadership of José María Vélaz (1843–1902) set about publishing a critical edition of the full correspondence of Saint Ignatius and other documents coming from his hand, such as the *Exercises* and the *Constitutions*. The first of the twelve volumes of Ignatius's correspondence rolled off the presses in 1894. The correspondence revealed Ignatius as a farsighted leader, a man altogether different from the prevailing stereotype of him as a martinet enforcer of military discipline in the army of Jesuit crusaders.

The correspondence was the first product in what developed into the series *Moumenta Historica Societatis Iesu*, a project that has grown into well over 150 volumes of texts, principally correspondence, from the early decades of the Society. The editors, all of them Jesuits until very recently, believed that making such documents available was the best means of refuting the calumnies against the Society, but the project also dispelled pious myths and led to a rediscovery of aspects of the Jesuit tradition that the overlay of centuries had obscured. It revealed a richer and more complex story in which adaptation to circumstances was characteristic. Study of these texts resulted in a less literal and moralistic reading of normative texts, including the *Spiritual Exercises*. When in 1925 the Spanish Jesuits founded the periodical *Manresa*, they began to make the results of their research available to a wider public.

Thus, as part of this historical revival, Jesuit historians turned their attention to the spirituality of the Society, now revealed in a new way. Perhaps the most influential of such scholars was Joseph de Guibert (1877–1942), a founder of the groundbreaking *Diction-naire de spiritualité*, 17 volumes (1937–1995). His influential *La spir-itualité de la Compagnie de Jésus* (published posthumously, 1953) was the first such survey ever attempted. By showing that Ignatius was truly a mystic, de Guibert helped reverse the trend that saw in the *Spiritual Exercises* (and hence in Jesuit spirituality) a recipe only for "strengthening the will" in order to achieve moral rectitude. When the French Jesuits in 1954 founded *Christus*, a journal dedi-cated to research and reflection on the Jesuit spiritual tradition, another decisive point had been reached.

By the end of World War II in 1945, therefore, the Jesuit and the larger Catholic cultural scene was much different from what it had been even a few decades earlier. The old antagonism between the church and Liberalism now seemed an outmoded dichotomy. As information about the horrors of the Holocaust became ever more vivid and undeniable, it provoked profound soul-searching about how Catholics thought and acted toward people of other faiths. The sometimes violent anti-colonialism that erupted around the world after World War II not only destroyed empires but forced Jesuits and others to reexamine the whole missionary enterprise.

Amid these and the other great cultural shifts evolving in mid-century, the Society of Jesus seemed to be faring well. In 1965 it counted some 36,000 members, the largest number in its history. Moreover, in the old mission lands the percentage of Jesuits who were native to the place was now considerable—50 percent, for instance, in the Philippines and Indonesia. The Society ran or was otherwise intrinsically related to more than 4,500 schools, with more than 50,000 non-Jesuit teachers and administrators and more than a million and a quarter students. In the United States alone the Jesuits conducted more than fifty secondary schools and twenty-eight at the tertiary level. In every province the Jesuits operated retreat houses and staffed thriving churches.

But there were problems. None was more troubling than that Eastern Europe and important mission fields such as China, North Korea, and Vietnam had fallen into Communist hands. The Jesuits in those places suffered greatly. When they were not forcibly expelled, they were often beaten, otherwise physically abused, and cast into prison to languish there without trial. Those not imprisoned had to go underground and were almost entirely cut off from communication with the rest of the Society.

In western Europe, after a large influx of new members into the Society immediately after World War II, the numbers had slacked off considerably by 1950, and in no countries more notably and surprisingly than in France and Italy. Virtually every religious order as well as the diocesan clergy suffered the same way. This was a problem, moreover, that had long afflicted Jesuit provinces in Latin America. By the time Vatican Council II opened in 1962, talk about "the vocation crisis" was common. Explanations for it were multiple, none fully satisfactory. However, leading the list was "the times," that is, an increasingly secularized society. The decline in vocations, the first since the restoration of the Society in 1814, turned out to be a trend that has continued to the present. By 1970 it had begun to be felt even in the United States, a country that until then had been immune to it.

THE ARRUPE ERA

The Second Vatican Council (1962–1965), an extraordinarily complex event, was in large part the Catholic Church's attempt to deal with the new cultural and religious situation that had long been in the making. The Council's decisions had a profound impact on Catholicism around the world and of course on the Society of Jesus. In 1964, just as the Council drew to a close, the superior general, Jean-Baptiste Janssens, died, an event that required the convocation of a General Congregation to elect his successor. As everybody realized, the Congregation, the thirty-first in the Society's history, would also have to provide the Society with guidance as to how to implement the decisions of the Council that affected both the Society's ministries and its internal life.

Before the Congregation's slightly more than two hundred delegates from around the world moved to that large agenda, they had to elect a new superior general. On the third ballot, their choice fell on a Spanish Basque, Pedro Arrupe, fifty-eight years old. At the time of his election he was provincial of the Japanese province, where he had been working for the past twenty-six years. When in 1945 the Americans dropped the bomb on Hiroshima, Arrupe was living in a Jesuit community just outside the city. Because of his skill and devotion in aiding those injured by the explosion, he excited widespread admiration. The devastation resulting from the bomb was an experience that marked him for life and gave him a profound revulsion at violence in any form.

As a young man Arrupe had trained for a medical career but interrupted it in 1927 to enter the Society. When a few years later the Spanish government exiled the Jesuits, Arrupe was forced to pursue the rest of his Jesuit training outside Spain, which he did in Belgium, Germany, Holland, and the United States. The delegates to the Thirty-First General Congregation had chosen, therefore, a man of cosmopolitan background and broad experience, precisely the kind of man needed to guide the Society in the unsettled times that were the late 1960s and 1970s.

Unlike previous generals, Arrupe traveled widely, visiting Jesuit communities in every part of the world. More Jesuits met him personally and heard him speak than was true of any previous general, including Saint Ignatius. Although he became perhaps the most beloved and admired general of the Society with the exception of Ignatius, he also had severe critics in the hierarchy and even in a few Jesuit circles, especially in Spain and in Rome itself.

The Congregation undertook a thorough review of every aspect of Jesuit life, and it did so in the light of what it called in its first decree the profound "social and cultural transformations" of the contemporary world. In an implementation of the Council, it issued for the first time in history a decree on ecumenism that encouraged Jesuits to become involved in the movement and to promote understanding among all religious traditions—something that earlier would have seemed impossible for a group of men popularly known as sworn enemies of the Reformation.

The Congregation reviewed the whole process by which Jesuits were trained. It made recommendations as to how they could be made more responsive to modern needs but also more in accord with the early traditions of the Society that the new scholarship was making clear. Vatican II in its decree *Perfectae caritatis* had bidden religious orders to make such an examination of their origins. It was an examination that had been under way in the Society for some time, but the Congregation now made some of its results officially operative.

In response to serious questions some Jesuits raised about whether the schools were worth the effort and were as effective in accomplishing the Society's mission as they were said to be, the

Congregation issued a long decree affirming their validity and recommending measures for their improvement. It also issued another important decree on the so-called social apostolate, whose purpose it defined as an endeavor "to build a fuller expression of justice and charity into the structures of human life." The Congregation further urged the Society "to devote its efforts" to parts of the world struggling with "hunger and other miseries of every sort." Individual Jesuits and groups of Jesuits had of course from the beginning of the order worked to this purpose, but the decree gave them and others a new impetus and encouragement. Father Arrupe himself later founded an organization that fulfilled this mandate in a specific way. By the late 1970s, he had become deeply concerned over the plight of the Vietnamese "boat people," who were clandestinely fleeing their homeland in highly risky sea voyages and seeking refuge any place that would accept them. It was particularly this situation that prompted him to take action. On November 14, 1980, he wrote to the Society announcing the establishment of the Jesuit Refugee Service as an official ministry of the Society.

The Service has in the meantime grown to a large and effective international organization under the direct authority of the general. Operative now in more than fifty countries, its mission is "to accompany, serve, and defend the rights of refugees and forcibly displaced persons." The Service, with a staff of about 75 Jesuits, 50 nuns, and 1,200 laypersons from all religious backgrounds, provides education, emergency relief, and psycho-social and pastoral services that every year reach over a half million refugees and others in distress.

When the Thirty-First General Congregation ended in 1966, nobody was prepared for the upheavals in the church and in the world that erupted just two years later, in 1968. No fully satisfactory explanation has emerged since then to explain the convergence of so many, such unexpected, and such peremptory public protests demanding often radical change in so many areas of life. In many parts of the globe, university students rioted, occupied classrooms and offices, and cried for changes of all kinds. Former colonies of European powers, even after they had ejected their former masters, were now often torn asunder by bloody internal conflicts. In the United States, the Civil Rights movement for equality for African Americans and the sometimes violent reaction to it had repercussions in other countries. Reaction against the war in Vietnam that the United States continued to wage excited violent protests against American foreign policy and ignited riots in countries far distant from the United States. In Italy, France, and elsewhere, Communist-inspired demonstrations and strikes paralyzed cities. The list could go on.

Although these and other upheavals of course had an impact upon the church and the Society, it was the so-called sexual revolution that hit them most directly, especially through the negative reaction to *Humane vitae*, Pope Paul VI's encyclical in 1968 on birth control. A number of theologians, priests, laypersons, and even bishops expressed dismay at the document and sometimes disagreement. A few Jesuits publicly criticized it. Others made clear they could not accept it and applied to leave the Society rather than be called upon to uphold it.

Meanwhile in Latin America bishops and theologians had for some years become ever more concerned about the plight and exploitation of the poor and about the injustice of the concentration of immense wealth in the hands of a minuscule percentage of the population to the detriment of the rest of society. They were critical of the church's failure effectively to address the problem. Out of this situation arose a form of reflection on the relationship between the Gospel and social issues that came to be known as liberation theology. Several Jesuits were prominent in developing its tenets, among which was the need for the church to play a much more proactive role in addressing social problems. Some theologians maintained the church had identified itself too closely with the interests of the wealthy and privileged classes.

Liberation theology deeply influenced decisions taken in 1968 at the extremely important meeting of the General Conference of Latin American Bishops in Medellín, Colombia.

Pedro Arrupe addressed the meeting and spoke in favor of the direction it was taking. Shortly after the meeting, however, some highly placed ecclesiastics took an extremely negative attitude toward the liberation-theology movement and accused it of being influenced by Marxist ideology, which was not entirely off the mark. In their minds, moreover, the Jesuits with Arrupe at their head had taken the lead in this dangerous and even unorthodox movement. Under Arrupe's leadership, they insisted, the Society had lost its bearings, as indicated by Jesuits' public criticism of the papacy and by the large numbers leaving the order.

It was against this background that Arrupe determined to convoke another General Congregation to meet in early December 1974. The avowed purpose of the Congregation was to review issues that had arisen since the Thirty-First Congregation and to finalize several important matters that that Congregation had consigned to commissions for study so that the next Congregation could make a better-informed decision on them. Understood but left unsaid was that the present Congregation was to be a referendum on Arrupe's leadership.

The question under the questions at the Congregation, therefore, was whether Arrupe was appropriately leading the Society. Unlike the Fifth General Congregation in 1593 that dealt with the leadership of Claudio Aquaviva, this Congregation never explicitly addressed the question. It did not need to. From the very first moment, the delegates made clear that they overwhelmingly approved of the direction Arrupe had given the Society and that he had their full support.

Nonetheless, the Thirty-Second General Congregation, which lasted three and a half months, turned out to be one of the most difficult in the whole history of the Society because of a series of unfortunate misunderstandings between it and Pope Paul VI. The criticisms of Arrupe had made their way into the Vatican and therefore to the pope. Complicated though the misunderstandings were, they can be reduced to two.

First, when the Congregation tried to change the stipulation in its legislation that only a restricted category of Jesuits could take part in the Society's governance at the higher levels, the pope and his advisers saw the attempt as an instance of the Jesuits' playing fast and loose with their traditions. At the audience with the delegates at the beginning of the Congregation, the pope communicated that he did not want a change, but he did so in opaque terms that seemed, at least to most of the delegates, to leave room for negotiation. The delegates were wrong. Their mistake led to a confused series of communications between the Congregation and the Vatican that gave the impression in the Vatican that the Jesuits felt free to disregard the clear wishes of the pope.

Even before the Congregation fully realized how determinedly opposed the pope was to the change in governance, a second cause of friction had emerged. In the provinces of the Society, the idea that the church and with it the Society should take a more active role in combating various forms of injustice in the world had taken hold. The provinces mandated the Congregation to deal with the issue.

The result of the Congregation's long and difficult debate over it resulted in a decree entitled "Our Mission Today: Service of Faith and Promotion of Justice." In a more compelling and explicit way than ever before in the Society's history, the decree committed the Society to struggle against violation of human rights. Even as the decree was being debated, certain quarters in Rome and in the Vatican saw the decree, like the liberation theology that was in part its inspiration, as tainted with Marxism and further indicative of the waywardness of the Jesuits under Arrupe. As the Congregation drew to a close, Paul VI let it be known that he wanted to review its decrees. Months later he finally gave approval even of the decree "Our Mission Today," but he was obviously still concerned.

In 1978, three years after the Congregation ended, Pope Paul was succeeded by Pope John Paul II. The new pope, though conventionally cordial to Arrupe, was from the beginning obviously wary about the leadership of the Society of Jesus. On August 7, 1981, Arrupe suffered a severe stroke, from which it soon became clear he could never fully recover. The *Constitutions* provided for such an eventuality by stipulating that a previously designated vicar step in to conduct business until a Congregation could be held to elect a new general. On October 6, 1981, the bomb dropped. Pope John Paul II informed the Jesuits that a new Congregation could not be held until he approved and, more shocking, that he had appointed his own vicar to replace the vicar Arrupe had designated before his illness, the American Vincent O'Keefe.

The pope's action, completely unexpected, stunned the Jesuits and left them confused and fearful about what it might ultimately mean for the Society. Was it perhaps, as some direly predicted, a prelude to another papal suppression of the order? As his vicar for the Society, the pope chose an experienced and respected Italian Jesuit, Paolo Dezza. The Jesuits soon began to realize that from their perspective John Paul could not have chosen a better man. With a gentle yet firm hand, he guided the Society and was able to quiet the Jesuits' worst fears. More important, he was able to persuade the pope that the Society was not the hotbed of rebellion its enemies had portrayed. Some of the enemies had predicted that the pope's intervention would spark a massive exodus of Jesuits from the Society, and they seem to have convinced the pope that he should expect that outcome. Nothing of the sort happened.

In a little over a year from the date of his intervention, John Paul gave permission for the convocation of a Congregation to elect a new general, and in so doing he restored the Society to its normal mode of government. The crisis, severe though it was, was short-lived. The Thirty-Third General Congregation opened on September 2, 1983, and the next day the delegates formally approved Arrupe's resignation. They then invited him, crippled and unable to speak, to join them for a few moments in the hall where they were meeting. When he appeared a thunderous applause broke out that went on for minute after minute, as if it would never end. The delegates thus bade farewell to a man they had come to admire and love, a man many of them considered a saint.

Events then moved quickly. A few days later, in another unprecedented move, Pope John Paul II let it be known that he wanted to come to the Jesuit curia to celebrate mass there for the delegates. His misgivings, the visit said, had been laid to rest. A few days later the delegates on the first ballot elected the Dutch Jesuit Peter-Hans Kolvenbach as the twenty-ninth general of the Society. Kolvenbach soon came to be deeply respected by the Jesuits and by the others with whom he dealt, who were consistently impressed by his wit, his straight talk, and his realistic assessment of situations and personalities.

MOVING TOWARD THE PRESENT

In 2008, after twenty-five years as general, during which cordial relations generally prevailed with the Vatican, Kolvenbach resigned. It was time, he said, for new leadership. He was succeeded by Adolfo Nicolás, a Spaniard who like Arrupe before him had spent his adult years in Japan as well as other parts of East Asia, where he held many responsible positions.

Jesuits had in the meantime taken seriously the responsibility that General Congregation Thirty-Two imposed upon them to be more active in trying to alleviate poverty and injustice, especially in parts of the world where those ills were more prevalent. They sometimes did so at the risk of their lives. Between 1975 and 2006, forty-six Jesuits died violent deaths, most of which occurred because their efforts in trying to improve the situation brought them into conflict with vested interests.

In 1989 in El Salvador occurred the most shocking of the assassinations. The country was in the midst of a bloody and vicious civil war. The government and its military correctly suspected the Jesuits at the Jesuit university of sympathizing with the rebels. Although they knew better, they accused them of storing weapons for the rebels and training guerrillas. In the early hours of the morning of November 16, commandos of the Salvadoran army entered the campus and brutally murdered six Jesuits, including the president of the university. To ensure there were no witnesses, they also murdered the Jesuits' cook and her daughter who were sleeping in a nearby room.

The military's attempt to blame the assassinations on the guerrillas proved impossible to sustain. As the killings began to be reported in the media outside El Salvador, they sparked an outrage that applied international pressure to learn who the killers were. In the end, the scandal of the murders helped speed negotiations and consolidate the peace.

Most Jesuit efforts to help those in need or distress such as the Jesuit Refugee Service took place without drama and public attention. In 1995, for instance, the American Jesuit John P. Foley founded in Chicago the first Cristo Rey school for disadvantaged boys and girls to enable them later to enter a university. The experiment succeeded, and in the next fifteen years Christo Rey schools grew to twenty-five spread across the United States. In cooperation with local businesses and government agencies, the students engage in a closely monitored work-study program. They work in law firms, banks, hospitals, universities, and business offices. The revenue generated from their work is the primary source for the funding of the school, which is open to students of all religious, ethnic, and cultural backgrounds. Virtually one hundred percent of the graduates are accepted into a tertiary-level school.

Older and incomparably more extensive is *Fe y Alegría*. In 1955 the Jesuit José María Vélaz (1910–1985) set out to create in Venezuela an effective program for the education of the country's most deprived children. He thereby launched the spectacularly successful *Fe y Alegría*, whose purpose is to promote through education a more just society in which all members are capable of participating constructively. Today in almost every country in Spanish America as well as in Spain, Chad, and elsewhere, it enrolls almost a million persons in at least one of its many programs. The network consists in more than 2,000 centers in which some 2,500 service units function, including a thousand school plants and sixty-seven radio stations. A Jesuit acts as coordinator for the International Federation of *Fe y Alegría*.

Even with such initiatives, the Jesuits continued to do what they in one form or another had been doing since the beginning. By far the largest percentage of Jesuits around the world are still engaged in education. In 2013 there were 189 Jesuit universities or other postsecondary schools around the world and a much larger number of secondary schools. In South Asia alone (primarily India), the Jesuits are responsible for 229 secondary schools plus another 164 primary and middle schools. Many Jesuits are of course engaged in traditional pastoral work in churches, hospitals, retreat houses, and similar institutions.

In the period between 1945 and 2000, the Jesuits entered another important era in their history as a missionary order. Members of the Society from every so-called developed country went in notable numbers to various parts of the world. The earlier missions to Africa stabilized, and new ones opened, with considerable success. In 1946, for instance, French Jesuits arrived in Chad and Cameroun, the seed from which the Province of West Africa was formed in 1983. The province today has about 255 members. The first Jesuits arrived in 1947 for the beginning of what developed into the Province of East Africa, which now numbers about 190 members. The other two African provinces have had similar patterns of growth. In 1960, India, until relatively recently considered a "mission country," had so prospered as to be able to send missionaries to Tanzania and shortly thereafter to the Sudan.

Since then India has continued to send Jesuits abroad in ever growing numbers to help others. In East Asia, Korea stands out as another success story. Jesuits from the United States came there only in 1960. Korea is now a province with almost two hundred members, virtually all of them Korean. Sogang University in Seoul, founded almost as soon as the Jesuits arrived, has achieved a distinguished reputation.

By the turn of the millennium, therefore, many lands once considered missions had matured into full-fledged provinces. As those provinces have grown, membership in the provinces that originally founded them has decreased. The decline in membership that first occurred in the 1950s in a few countries of western Europe continued and, as mentioned, meanwhile spread to others. By 2010 the Jesuits were about half as many as they were at the peak year of 1965. In Europe and the United States/Canada, the drop in the number of men entering the Society has been considerable, whereas the number entering in other parts of the world, though sometimes relatively small, has grown or remained stable. The areas of growth have been Africa and Asia, most especially India.

Thus the proportion of men entering the Society in different parts of the world has reversed from what it was several decades ago when by far the greatest number of new Jesuits came from the developed world. This demographic shift is one of the most significant changes in the history of the Society since its origins. In recent years some 75 percent of new recruits have come from outside Europe and North America. If this trend continues, for the first time in the Society's long history, the overwhelming majority of Jesuits will be from Africa and Asia. The Society of Jesus, a global institution from its first moment, will become at that point a global institution in an altogether different way.

On March 13, 2013, the cardinals of the Roman Catholic Church stunned the world by electing as pope the Argentinean Jorge Mario Bergoglio—a Jesuit, the first Jesuit pope in history! Upon his election the members of the Society were as utterly surprised by the choice as was everybody else and perhaps more so. They in no way anticipated that one of their own number might be chosen. Whether that event will have any direct impact on the Society remains to be seen. Nonetheless, having a Jesuit as pope, an eventuality that through the centuries seemed almost unthinkable, might somehow open a new page in the history of the Society of Jesus.

EPILOGUE: LOOKING BACK AND LOOKING AHEAD

I realize these pages have done little more than glide over the surface of a long and complex history, yet I hope the journey has resulted in a somewhat better understanding of those mysterious creatures, the Jesuits. But the mystery has not been altogether dispelled. The history of the Society of Jesus is not only rich and complex; it is *extraordinarily* rich and complex. It stretches over centuries, continents, and cultures, in which the Jesuits have played a strikingly wide range of roles.

For that reason the Jesuits resist easy categorization. They are priests but also astronomers. They pledge obedience yet are encouraged to cultivate initiative. They pronounce a solemn vow to be missionaries, yet the largest percentage of them even today are resident schoolmasters. Although they have a reputation for cultivating the high-born and have been the confessors of kings, they have consistently devised means of reaching every stratum of society, with a special concern for the most wretched.

The Jesuits have provoked fear and envy in ways and to a degree not verified in any other Catholic religious order. The phenomenon has produced a large stream of vituperation, at the headwaters of which are the *Monita Secreta* and the *Lettres Provinciales*. Such works created myths and misunderstandings about the Jesuits that entered so deeply into the public domain that they seem impossible to eradicate. In virtually every Western language the adjective *jesuitical* means devious, slippery, sinister.

Even for the fair-minded the Jesuits can be difficult to understand because of the changes the order has undergone over the course of the centuries. Some changes were the result of deliberate decisions of the members, some the result of forces from outside. Even such a brief book as this has provided examples of both types of change.

Some of those changes are of course more important than others. In the history of the Society, four are undoubtedly pivotal. Each of them has marked a significant moment in Jesuit self-definition that was at the same time a partial redefinition of the Society. These moments were turning points. A more dramatic way to express the phenomenon is to say that the Society has several times refounded itself. Although each refounding has drawn its core identity from the past, it has partially reshaped the past or moved beyond it. If we adopt the conceit of a prologue and four foundings to organize the history of the Society of Jesus, the following is the result.

THE PROLOGUE

In 1534 Ignatius and six other students at the University of Paris pronounced a vow of poverty and determined to travel together

to the Holy Land. They were no longer simply students who associated with one another; they were now bonded together in a
common enterprise. Though they were not aware of it, they at
that moment took the first step that would lead to the official
founding of the Society. Before they left Paris they were joined by
three other students. They began to describe themselves as members of a *compagnia di Gesù*, a brotherhood of Jesus.

THE FIRST FOUNDING

In 1540 the companions of Paris now bound themselves together
permanently as members of a religious order, formally recognized
as such by the church. This meant they replaced their informal
and egalitarian lifestyle with that of members of an organization
with *Constitutions*, procedures, superiors, and subjects. From a
close-knit band of ten friends, they had grown by the death of
Ignatius to a membership a hundred times larger.

THE SECOND FOUNDING

Sometime around 1550 Ignatius, in consultation with his closest
advisers, took the momentous step of committing the Society to
formal schooling as its primary ministry. This was a decision of
immense import for the future of Catholicism but more immediately for the Society of Jesus. The original ideal of a band of missionaries and itinerant preachers now had to be modified to take
account of the Society as also a band of resident schoolmasters.
Moreover, Ignatius's decision wrought a profound change in the

culture of the Society, as Jesuits became specialists in every branch of knowledge and every cultural form, including theater, music, and dance.

THE THIRD FOUNDING

By virtue of the papal brief of 1773, the Society of Jesus had ceased to exist. By virtue of a papal bull forty-one years later, it was restored to life. The Society was restored as part of a wave of conservative restorations initiated in that year, 1814, and its self-understanding began to reflect that fact. In its essential identity it was the same Society as before the suppression, yet its cultural, political, and even religious mind-set reflected the culture of restoration prevalent in Catholicism in this period.

THE FOURTH FOUNDING

General Congregation Thirty-One, 1965–1966, made its decisions under the influence of two powerful factors that no previous Congregation had had to take into account. The first was the cumulative effect upon Jesuit self-understanding of the intense study of Jesuit sources that had been under way for the previous half-century. That study had resulted in an understanding of the early Society and its normative documents that was more flexible and less moralistic than the understanding generally operative since the restoration in 1814.

The second was Vatican Council II, which ended just as the Congregation was beginning. The Congregation saw its major task as implementing for the Society the ideals and vision of the council. It gave the Society the mandate, for instance, to promote understanding and dialogue among people of all religious faiths. It in more general terms took account of the great cultural shifts that had occurred since the restoration of 1814 and moved the Society beyond certain positions it had formally or informally adopted in those circumstances.

In the meantime the four Congregations that have subsequently taken place have directed the Society along those same lines. What is clear is that the Society is now evolving in new ways in a world that seems to be evolving even faster. Its challenge now, as always, is to retain its identity while at the same time exploiting its tradition of adaptation to persons, places, and circumstances.

There is reason to believe the identity will hold. Through all the changes over the years, the Jesuits have had to guide them some remarkable resources that have continued to be their touchstones for authenticity. Absolutely primary among them are the *Spiritual Exercises*, the *Formula*, and the *Constitutions*. While each of these documents counsels flexibility and adaptability, the principles that undergird them are firm. They provide the foundation for an identity that in its general contours is discernible by an alert eye.

FURTHER READING

The quantity of literature on the Jesuits is overwhelming. Although earlier writings about them often still have merit, most are marred by either apologetic or polemical concerns. About the middle of the last century that situation began gradually to change, but only in the past twenty years have studies of the Jesuits for the most part altogether shaken off those prejudices and in other ways entered an entirely new phase. The Jesuits currently excite more interest among scholars of almost every discipline than ever before, and they do so on an international basis. I limit myself here to a highly selective sampling of works written in English.

GENERAL HISTORIES: MONOGRAPHS

Arrupe, Pedro. *One Jesuit's Spiritual Journey: Autobiographical Conversations with Jean-Claude Dietsch.* Saint Louis, MO: The Institute of Jesuit Sources, 1986.

An important testimony from one of the Society's most important superiors general.

Bangert, William V. *A History of the Society of Jesus*. Saint Louis, MO: The Institute of Jesuit Sources, 1972.

Although somewhat outdated, the most thorough and reliable treatment.

Lacouture, Jean. *Jesuits: A Multibiography*. Trans. Jeremy Leggatt. Washington, DC: Counterpoint, 1995.

A lively but selective account by a leading French journalist and biographer.

Padberg, John W. *The General Congregations of the Society of Jesus: A Brief Survey of Their History*. Saint Louis, MO: American Assistancy Seminar on Jesuit Spirituality, 1974.

The best account of the central component of Jesuit governance, to be complemented by Padberg's later study of the recent Congregations.

GENERAL HISTORIES: COLLECTIONS

O'Malley, John W., et al., eds. *The Jesuits; Cultures, Sciences, and the Arts, 1540–1773*. Toronto: University of Toronto Press, 1999.

Together with a further volume published in 2006, impressive studies on a wide range of topics related to the Jesuits and cultural issues.

Worcester, Thomas, ed. *The Cambridge Companion to the Jesuits*. Cambridge and New York: Cambridge University Press, 2008.

This volume complements the Toronto volumes with topics more related to the institutional history of the order. It includes a bibliography.

FOUNDATIONS

Brodrick, James. *Saint Peter Canisius*. Chicago, IL: Loyola University Press, 1962.

Originally published in 1935, this biography of one of the order's most important members is outdated and hagiographical but still basic and unsurpassed.

Dalmases, Cándido de. *Ignatius of Loyola, Founder of the Jesuits: His Life and Work.* Trans. Jerome Aixalá. Saint Louis, MO: The Institute of Jesuit Sources, 1985.

On the pious side, but impeccably reliable in factual details.

Lazar, Lance Gabriel. *Working in the Vineyard of the Lord: Jesuit Confraternities in Early Modern Italy.* Toronto: University of Toronto Press, 2005.

A careful study of a generally unrecognized but important enterprise of Ignatius and the other Jesuits of that generation.

O'Malley, John W. *The First Jesuits.* Cambridge, MA: Harvard University Press, 1993.

The standard work on the first generation of Jesuits.

Tellechea Idígoras, José Ignacio. *Ignatius of Loyola, the Pilgrim Saint.* Trans. Cornelius Michael Buckley. Chicago, IL: Loyola University Press, 1994.

A lively, somewhat romantic biography by a distinguished Spanish historian.

ANTI-JESUIT WRITINGS

Burke, Peter. "The Black Legend of the Jesuits: An Essay in the History of Historical Stereotypes." In Simon Ditchfield, ed., *Christianity and Community in the West: Essays for John Bossy.* Aldershot: Ashgate, 2001, 165–82.

An overview of the problem by a distinguished historian.

Maryks, Robert Aleksander. *Saint Cicero and the Jesuits: The Influence of the Liberal Arts on the Adoption of Moral Probabilism.* Aldershot: Ashgate, 2008.

An interesting study of this important aspect of the culture of the Society of Jesus, which concludes with a chapter on the Jansenist offensive against probabilism.

Pavone, Sabina. *The Wiley Jesuits and the Monita Secreta: The Forged Secret Instructions of the Jesuits: Myth and Reality.* Trans. John P. Murphy. Saint Louis, MO: The Institute of Jesuit Sources, 2004.

The standard study of one of the most damaging and long-lived attacks on the Jesuits, which includes an English version of the original text.

THE JESUITS AND POLITICS

Bireley, Robert. *The Jesuits and the Thirty Years War: Kings, Courts, and Confessors.* Cambridge and New York: Cambridge University Press, 2003.
A masterly study of one of the most contentious aspects of Jesuit history, Jesuit confessors to kings.

Nelson, Eric. *The Jesuits and the Monarchy: Catholic Reform and Political Authority in France (1590–1615).* Aldershot: Ashgate, 2005.
The story of the difficult time the Jesuits had in establishing themselves in France.

Shore, Paul. *Jesuits and the Politics of Religious Pluralism in Eighteenth-Century Transylvania: Culture, Politics and Religion, 1693–1773.* Aldershot: Ashgate, 2007.
A wide-ranging study of the Jesuits in a complex sector of the Habsburg empire.

Van Kley, Dale. *The Jansenists and the Expulsion of the Jesuits from France, 1757–1765.* New Haven, CT: Yale University Press, 1975.
Still the best study of the pivotal event in the history of the Jesuits.

THE JESUITS WORLDWIDE

Alden, Daurel. *The Making of an Enterprise: The Society of Jesus in Portugal, Its Empire, and Beyond, 1540–1750.* Stanford, CA: Stanford University Press, 1996.
A sweeping account of the Jesuits' relationship to their most important patron nation.

Brockey, Liam Matthew. *Journey to the East: The Jesuit Mission to China, 1579–1724.* Cambridge, MA: Harvard University Press, 2007.
Award-winning study of the Jesuits not in Beijing but out in the field.

Clossey, Luke. *Salvation and Globalization in the Early Jesuit Missions.* Cambridge and New York: Cambridge University Press, 2008.
Presents the missions not as a disjointed collection of individual entities but as a single, world-encompassing instance of religious globalization.

Cushner, Nicholas P. *Why Have You Come Here? The Jesuits and the Evangeli-zation of Native America*. Oxford and New York: Oxford University Press, 2006.

Covers the Jesuits' efforts with the native peoples from Canada to Para-guay.

Hsia, Ronnie Po-chia. *A Jesuit in the Forbidden City: Matteo Ricci, 1552–1610*. Oxford and New York: Oxford University Press, 2010.

A readable account of this legendary figure and a good introduction to the Beijing mission.

Klaiber, Jeffrey. *The Jesuits In Latin America, 1549–2000: 450 Years of Incultur-ation, Defense of Human Rights, and Prophetic Witness*. St Louis, MO: The Institute of Jesuit Sources, 2009.

The basic story from beginning to the present, told with a specific focus.

Mkenda, Festo. *Mission for Everyone: A Story of the Jesuits in Eastern Africa (1555–2012)*. Nairobi: Paulines Publications Africa, 2013.

The only comprehensive account in English of the Jesuits in any region of Africa.

THE ENGLISH-SPEAKING WORLD

Curran, Robert Emmett. *The Maryland Jesuits, 1634–1833*. Baltimore: The Corporation of Roman Catholic Clergymen, Maryland Province of the Society of Jesus, 1976.

An account of the first Jesuits to make a permanent settlement in what would become the United States.

McCoog, Thomas M. *"And Touching our Society": Fashioning Jesuit Identity in Elizabethan England*. Toronto: Pontifical Institute of Mediaeval Studies, 2013.

The latest book by the expert on the Jesuits in the British Isles.

McKevitt, Gerald. *Brokers of Culture: Italian Jesuits in the American West, 1848–1919*. Stanford, CA: Stanford University Press, 2007.

Fascinating story of the first Jesuits in the far west.

Schroth, Raymond A. *The American Jesuits: A History*. New York: New York
University Press, 2007.
An accessible account of the Society in the United States.

THE SCHOOLS

Curran, Robert Emmett. *A History of Georgetown University*. 3 vols. Washington, DC: Georgetown University Press, 2010.
A detailed account of the first Catholic school on American soil.
Grendler, Paul F. *The University of Mantua, the Gonzaga, and the Jesuits, 1584–1630*. Baltimore, MD: The Johns Hopkins University Press, 2009.
The only in-depth study in English of a Jesuit pre-suppression school, by the expert on schooling in early modern Italy.
Padberg, John W. *Colleges in Controversy: The Jesuit Schools in France from Revival to Suppression, 1815–1880*. Cambridge, MA: Harvard University Press, 1969.
The best account of schools on the continent after the restoration of the Society.

SCIENCE

Feingold, Modechai, ed. *Jesuit Science and the Republic of Letters*. Cambridge, MA: MIT Press, 2003.
An impressive collection of articles about the Jesuits' contributions to science.
Findlen, Paula. *Athanasius Kircher: The Last Man Who Knew Everything*. London: Routledge, 2004.
The story of the famous Jesuit eccentric and his accomplishments.
Helyer, Marcus. *Catholic Physics: Jesuit Natural Philosophy in Early Modern Germany*. Notre Dame, IN: University of Notre Dame Press, 2005.
The story of how the Jesuits came to adopt modern methods in science.

Wallace, William. *Galileo and His Sources: The Heritage of the Collegio Romano in Galileo's Science.* Princeton: Princeton University Press, 1984.
How the Jesuits influenced Galileo, told by an eminent historian of science.

THE ARTS

Bailey, Gauvin Alexander. *Art on the Jesuit Missions in Asia and Latin America, 1542–1773.* Toronto: University of Toronto Press, 1999.
Award-winning account that begins in Europe and sweeps through the rest of the world.

Celenza, Anna Harwell, and Anthony R. DelDonna, eds. *Music as Cultural Mission: Explorations of Jesuit Practices in Italy and North America.* Philadelphia, PA: Saint Joseph's University Press, 2014.
A window into the world of Jesuit music production, practices, and patronage.

McCabe, William. *An Introduction to the Jesuit Theater.* Ed. Louis Oldani. Saint Louis, MO: The Institute of Jesuit Sources, 1985.
This posthumous work is somewhat outdated but still the best general work on the subject in English.

O'Malley, John W., and Gauvin Alexander Bailey, eds. *The Jesuits and the Arts, 1540–1773.* Philadelphia, PA: Saint Joseph's University Press, 2005.
A sumptuously produced volume covering Jesuit artistic enterprises worldwide.

Rock, Judith. *Terpsichore at Louis-le-Grand: Baroque Dance and the Jesuit Stage in Paris.* Saint Louis, MO: The Institute of Jesuit Sources, 1996.
The best introduction in English to the history of Jesuit dance.

NOTES

PREFACE

1. This and all subsequent citations are from the series *Monumenta Historica Societatis Iesu*. *Monumenta Nadal*, 5:364–65.

CHAPTER 1: FOUNDATIONS

1. *Monumenta Ignatiana, Epistolae*, 12:310.
2. *Monumenta Nadal*, 4:215.
3. *Monumenta Nadal*, 5:773–74.
4. See Serafim Leite, *História da Companhia de Jesus no Brasil*, 10 vols. (Lisbon: Livraria Portugália, 1938–1950), 2:282n5.
5. *Fontes Narativi*, 1:581–82.

CHAPTER 2:
THE FIRST HUNDRED YEARS

1. *Epistolae S. Francisci Xaverii*, 2:179–212n12.

INDEX

ABOUT THE AUTHOR

John W. O'Malley, SJ, currently university professor in the theology department of Georgetown University, is a church historian whose specialty is sixteenth- and seventeenth-century Europe. Among his best-known books are *The First Jesuits*, *Trent and All That*, *Four Cultures of the West*, *What Happened at Vatican II*, *A History of the Popes*, and *Trent*. *The First Jesuits*, translated into ten languages, won both the Jacques Barzun Prize for cultural history and the Philip Schaff Prize for church history. John O'Malley was elected to the American Academy of Arts and Sciences in 1995 and to the American Philosophical Society in 1997. He is past president of the American Catholic Historical Association and the Renaissance Society of America. A Catholic priest and member of the Society of Jesus, Father O'Malley has received lifetime achievement awards from the Renaissance Society of America, the Society for Italian Historical Studies, and the American Catholic Historical Association.